MY
GOOD FRIEND
THE
RATTLESNAKE

MY GOOD FRIEND
THE
RATTLESNAKE

LESSONS OF LOSS, TRUTH, AND TRANSFORMATION

DON JOSE RUIZ
New York Times **Bestselling Coauthor of *The Fifth Agreement***

with TAMI HUDMAN

Hierophantpublishing

Cover design by Adrian Morgan
Cover art by istockphoto and Shutterstock

Print book interior design by Frame25 Productions

Hierophant Publishing
San Antonio, TX
www.hierophantpublishing.com

If you are unable to order this book from your local bookseller, you may order directly from the publisher.

Library of Congress Control Number: 2024946488
ISBN 978-1-950253-49-4

10 9 8 7 6 5 4 3 2 1

To all who are trapped in the addiction to suffering. Remember that there is always a path to return to your true home.

Contents

Foreword by don Miguel Ruiz   ix

Introduction   1

1. Baby Rattlesnake   11

2. Shedding Skins   21

3. The Illusion of Judgment   31

4. Attention, Intention, Action   41

5. Being Given a Spiritual Name   51

6. Stepping into My Dream   61

7. The Barrio Buddha   71

8. Crossing the Border   81

9. A Trip to Egypt   91

10. Heavy Metal   105

11. Welcoming Home the Love of My Life   115

12. The Fallen Messenger   125

13. The Burning Candle   135

14. The Courage to Act   145

15. The Eternal Honeymoon   155

Conclusion   165

Foreword

The story of don Jose's life really begins nine months before his birth. He has no recollection of this part, but I do. It was just before Christmas, 1977, and I was in my last year of medical school at the University of Mexico. My wife and I had traveled to San Diego with our young son, Miguel Jr., to spend the holidays with family. On Christmas Eve, we all gathered at my brother Jaime's house and spent a wonderful evening with my older brothers Luis and Carlos, who were also visiting from Mexico. In the middle of this happy reunion, though, I experienced a feeling of sadness. It was weird, but for some reason it felt like this might be the last Christmas of my life. I tried to put on a happy face because it was the holidays and I didn't want to darken the mood, but this feeling stayed with me through the rest of the trip.

After the holidays, we came home to Mexico City and I resumed my studies at the university. The mood there was festive as students looked forward to the end of the year and their upcoming internships. Toward the end of January, there was a big celebration in Cuernavaca. I borrowed a car from my brother Luis and drove down with a couple of my friends. It was a great party. We drank a lot that night, had lots of fun, and when the party was over, I made a decision that would change my life. Although my friends and I were intoxicated and tired, we decided to drive back to Mexico City. I drove very fast, wanting to get home before morning. We were laughing and joking, talking about our future as interns, when I was overwhelmed by fatigue. I fell asleep.

I woke up in the hospital the next day. When I asked what had happened, the nurse replied, "Don't you remember? You just killed your friends in a car crash!" I was shocked and ashamed, unable to hold back tears. "Sorry," she said quickly, seeing my reaction. "Nothing happened to them. They're alive and well. But," she added, "it's a miracle that the three of you are alive." Apparently, my two friends weren't even in the car at the moment of impact. I was driving, but I was also unharmed. Once I heard that, I began to remember the events of the night before.

I remembered seeing my body asleep at the wheel. I remembered the screams of my friends as they realized they were about to die, and I remembered opening the door and taking them both out of the car before we hit the wall. I remembered all of that, even as I knew my body was asleep in the driver's seat. I remembered embracing my body just before the crash, protecting it from injury. In those days, there were no such things as seat belts or airbags. The car was totaled, and yet we all survived. It was impossible to know how such a thing could happen; it really was a miracle.

I had to ask myself, *What am I?* That question sent me on a long journey of discovery away from my life as a medical doctor. Before that night, I had a theory that we are not the body, that we only live *within* the body — but it was just a theory. Now, lying in the hospital and recalling the details of the crash, that theory became a fact, at least for me. My perception completely changed. I had so many more questions, and I needed answers. I wanted the truth.

When I got home from the hospital, my wife was extremely happy. Of course, she was relieved that I was alive and uninjured, but she had also just found out that she was pregnant. The story of my son Jose Luis had begun before the holidays the previous month. My family's love, my revelations, and the shifts that resulted from the car crash were all part of the process of his creation. The events of the weeks after his conception were registered in my body, in my wife's body, and in the body of our unborn child.

If we use our imaginations, we can recognize the most important event of my son's life. It was a race where millions of sperm competed to fertilize an ovum. Only one of several hundred mature eggs was destined to receive the winner, and only one among millions of sperm was destined to achieve its goal. My son Jose was the winner early that December, and his reward was life. A sperm makes up half a cell; the ovum makes the other, and together they create one cell, which divides into countless cells to create a brand-new universe. This universe originates from the merging of two people, and it takes nine months to build. Like all parents, Maria and I created a unique human. There never was a human like him, nor will there ever be one again. Nine months after conception, a second miracle happened. On September 18, 1978, Jose was born.

My brother Carlos delivered him, and as he placed little Jose into my hands, I was deeply moved. At that moment, I felt as if I was holding myself in my hands. I recognized so much of myself in him. In his eyes I saw a new messenger, someone who would change the lives of countless people with his message of love. There are no words to describe the strong connection I felt to him, a connection that would remain throughout his childhood and that still exists between us today. I have experienced certain moments of Jose's life in my dreams, and in many cases, I've been unable to separate his feelings from my own.

Many events have shaped Jose and made him the man he is today. He has used all of his precious life experiences to become a true messenger of love, beginning with the events occurring before his birth. In this beautiful book, Jose will tell you many stories about his life and its important lessons.

I have just told you how the story of his life began.

—don Miguel Ruiz

Introduction

From the beginning of time, snakes have haunted the human imagination, representing a form of consciousness that some of us find sinister and alien, and others find awesome and wise. For many of us, the mere mention of snakes is enough to provoke fear. We instinctively recoil at the thought of these ancient and mysterious beings, with their associations of danger, violence, and the unknown.

Our fear of snakes is understandable, because many of us have been warned since childhood that these scaly creatures can cause us serious injury or even death. In my family's Toltec tradition, this is an example of a useful and positive form of *domestication*—a word that expresses the Toltec idea of how we humans are taught the rules of our society. If children were not warned that snakes bite, many tragedies would occur.

But for many people, especially in the Jewish, Christian, and Islamic traditions, fear and dislike of snakes is tied to cultural associations, and not simply to the physical danger they pose. Most of us are familiar with the story of Adam and Eve, in which a serpent's tricks are central to humankind's expulsion from the Garden of Eden, but there are many other examples in the Bible of snakes being demonized. From ancient Greece, often considered the birthplace of Western civilization, comes the story of Medusa, and how one look at her head of snakes would turn the viewer to stone. In Scottish lore, the *beithir* is a huge and terrifying snake who lives in secluded mountain caves, coming out of its lair to gobble up horses and give people deadly stings.

Fear of snakes isn't confined to the Abrahamic religions and Western mythology. In a well-known Buddhist story, the demon Mara, who comes to tempt Buddha while he sits in meditation under the

Bodhi tree, is also depicted as a serpent. An ancient collection of Japanese mythology called the Kojiki tells of the Yamata no Orochi, a snake with eight heads and eight tails who came down from the mountains once a year to eat young girls alive. From West to East, you can find stories associating snakes with the negative aspects of human experience.

But snakes weren't always painted in such a negative light. In ancient India, snakes called *nagas* were respected as the sacred guardians of temples; Buddha is sometimes represented with a cobra standing behind him to give him shade; and the so-called Snake Sutta in the Pali canon praises the skillfulness of monks who give up negative qualities like anger, greed, and craving as a snake gives up its old skin. Indigenous peoples in the Americas honor snakes for their qualities of regeneration and wisdom and for their connection to the underworld.

My family descended from the ancient Toltecs, who lived and prospered over two thousand years ago in what we now call south central Mexico. In the Toltec tradition, the most powerful deity was Quetzalcoatl, a feathered serpent combining the qualities of a bird and a rattlesnake. Indeed, the Toltec city of Teotihuacan is home to the Temple of the Feathered Serpent, a pyramid covered with carvings of this otherworldly being. Quetzalcoatl was a redeeming figure whose mission was to bring peace, love, and healing to our people.

Although Teotihuacan is the birthplace of Quetzalcoatl, there is substantial evidence that some version of the snake god was worshiped throughout most of North America. The Native American Hopi tribe has a snake dance that goes back thousands of years. Ohio's famous Serpent Mound, a stunning 1,300-foot-long earthwork structure in the shape of a slithering snake whose tail is coiled into a spiral, was built by native peoples more than a thousand years ago. When Europeans arrived in North America, they took the serpent mound to be a sign that their Christian god had marked this spot as the site of the Garden of Eden.

From a shamanic perspective, snakes have much to teach us. They shed their skin and leave it behind, renewing themselves over and over again, never clinging to one form. Although they may have venom or even poison at their disposal, they are masters of self-control and do not strike unless absolutely necessary. They are also masters of silence who do not dissipate their energy in thoughtless chatter, but observe life carefully and quietly; for this reason, many cultures associate them with wisdom.

Throughout my life, the rattlesnake has been a great teacher to me. Where I used to live in the mountains of San Diego, I had the opportunity to see a few rattlesnakes every spring and summer. I would spot them in the tall grass, where they hunted for mice; if I was lucky, I would find a delicate, nearly transparent piece of skin in some forgotten corner of my toolshed or under a tipped-over wheelbarrow. Finding a piece of rattlesnake skin always felt like a precious reminder that life is a never-ending cycle of resurrection.

I am no stranger to the concept of resurrection. Sometimes, it feels like my entire life has been one long series of rebirths. As I approach my fiftieth birthday, many people see me as a loving and carefree person with an open heart. "Oh, that Jose, he must have been born happy," they say. "Some people are just so lucky." They don't see all the skins I had to shed to arrive at the joyful place I am today. They don't know that for many years, I struggled in the darkness of the underworld, searching for the wisdom that would set me free.

Don Miguel Ruiz

My father, don Miguel Ruiz, plays a central role in my life and consequently in this book. For that reason, I would like to tell you a little more about him. Even though I call him Pops, the truth is that don Miguel is my teacher just as much as he is my father. He is a *nagual*, or shaman, in the Toltec tradition, just like his mother, Madre Sarita, his grandfather don Leonardo, and a long line of ancestors before them.

The Nahuatl word *Toltec* means artist, and the Toltec tradition teaches that we are the artists of our own lives, shaping our experience through the power of our words, actions, and beliefs. Toltec tradition also emphasizes the fact that humanity is dreaming, and waking up from the dream is central to becoming a nagual.

In his younger years, my father didn't want to become a shaman or *curandero* like his mother. Instead, he went to medical school and became a Western-style doctor, a surgeon. But after the fateful car crash he talks about in the foreword to this book, his interest in the Toltec tradition of our family was ignited. He also realized that Toltec teachings aren't meant to be practiced in exactly the same way from generation to generation—they are meant to evolve, to live and grow. He began teaching his own style of Toltec shamanism to small groups of apprentices. Indeed, many of my childhood memories are of sitting in on these classes, watching in awe as my father taught.

Still, my father didn't become famous until he published *The Four Agreements* when I was twenty years old. This book has gone on to sell millions of copies and transform millions of lives. People like Oprah Winfrey and Tom Brady have praised *The Four Agreements* for the simple yet powerful framework it provides for living an ethical, meaningful, and peaceful life.

Sometimes, people assume that because my father is a spiritual master I must have had an idyllic life, but this couldn't be further from the truth. In fact, my childhood and teenage years were filled with turmoil, and marked by traumas that took me many years to overcome. Regardless of my father's spiritual achievements, I had to undergo my own shamanic initiation, and pass through an underworld of my own devising, in order to become the person I am today.

How to Use This Book

I wrote this book to pierce through the illusion that unconditional love and inner peace are granted to the lucky few whose lives are untouched by trauma, abuse, addiction, and plain bad luck. In my case, I went through decades of darkness before slowly uncovering the light I held within. Ultimately, the darkness become my teacher, and the traumas I experienced gave rise to the immense love and gratitude I feel today. Now I too have become a nagual in the Eagle Knight lineage of my father and grandmother. Like a rattlesnake, I learned to shed my old skin and tap into my innate capacity for renewal.

My sincere hope is that this book will awaken that capacity in anyone who reads it. Along with sharing my personal story, I've included several tools as well as thirty exercises, which are designed to help you tap into the sacred wisdom of the rattlesnake—a wisdom as deep as is it timeless. You may choose to do the exercises in the order they are presented here, or you can pick and choose the ones that speak to you most at this particular moment in your life—it's up to you. I encourage you to consider trying each exercise at least once and repeat those that you find success with. It's through repetition and dedication that we make meaningful and lasting change in our lives.

Finally, I want to remind you that as you embark on this journey, no matter what you have done, how long you have spent in darkness, or how much trauma you have gone through, the best time to wake up from the dream is always right now. It is never too late to shed your skin, as rebirth is always waiting to emerge from beneath the old.

1

Baby Rattlesnake

Man learns through experience, and the spiritual path is full of different kinds of experiences. He will encounter many difficulties and obstacles, and they are the very experiences he needs to encourage and complete the cleansing process.

—Sai Baba

One of the most important things you learn when you live in rattlesnake country is that baby rattlesnakes are far more dangerous than adult ones. This is because when a rattlesnake is young, it hasn't yet developed the ability to control its poison. If a baby rattlesnake were to bite you, it would inject all its poison in one go, and you would be far more likely to die. Once a rattlesnake grows and becomes an adult, however, it learns to control its poison. If an adult were to bite you, it might only release a small amount. This makes your chances of survival much greater.

As a child and teenager, I had much in common with a baby rattlesnake. When I had an emotional reaction to something, I'd release all my poison at once—playing the victim, lashing out, or making a scene to get what I wanted. Just like a baby rattlesnake, I didn't think about the consequences of my actions—I only knew that releasing all my poison was the fastest way to feel safe.

My parents divorced when I was seven, and I lived with my mother in Tijuana, Mexico, while my father and older brother moved to San Diego, California. I soon learned to use my poison to manipulate both of my parents. I started skipping school, forging my mom's signature on the absent notices, and lying when she asked me where I'd been. Whenever I wanted my dad to visit from San Diego, I'd break something or cause some other mischief, so he would have to come and fix it. My mom worked the night shift and had a long commute. She also had my younger brother, Leonardo, to worry about. Try as she might, she simply wasn't able to keep a close enough eye on me to keep me out of trouble—and she'd learned to be wary of the poison I could unleash when she tried to set any rules.

By the time I was in my early teens, I had a job at my friend's dad's moving company, which meant I had money of my own to spend as I pleased. I was like a stray cat, coming home only when I was hungry, or when I needed a safe place to sleep off the partying I'd done with my friends the night before. Thanks to my parents' divorce and my mom's work schedule, I had a great deal of physical freedom—and I took advantage of that freedom to run the streets with my friends.

When I was fifteen, my mom decided to move to San Diego so she could be closer to work. When she told me we were moving to America, I hit the roof. "There's no way I'm moving there!" I said. "I don't even speak English. And I wouldn't last one day at that preppy high school with Miguel." I told her I was staying behind in Tijuana—and I wouldn't take no for an answer. When my mother raised concerns about me staying behind, I simply unleashed more poison until she was exhausted.

At first, living alone in Tijuana was a blast. My newly empty house quickly became the go-to party spot, where my friends and I could drink, smoke weed, and crank our music all night long. Before we knew it, we'd even made some new friends—older, tougher guys who showed up to party, and who offered us crystal meth. Snorting meth made us feel energized and creative, our minds overflowing with brilliant ideas for art and music. In those early days, meth felt so innocent. We weren't addicts, but bohemians living each day like it was our last.

But soon, the dark side made itself known: I found myself craving meth, and needing more and more of it to stave off the terrible feelings of withdrawal that overcame me when my high wore off. I would wake up in the morning thinking about how

I would get my next fix. Meanwhile, the house was becoming filthier and filthier, its carpets trampled by a never-ending stream of shoes. Somehow, I never seemed to get around to cleaning—it was always more important to track down some meth before I did anything else.

My parents both sensed that something was off, but just like a rattlesnake, I was an expert at camouflage. When either of them came to visit, I would make myself presentable, chatting about school and my job at the moving company, explaining that I was just too busy to clean. In Mexican culture it's considered normal for teenagers to drink, so I would sometimes let them think I was hungover. But if anyone challenged me or asked too many questions, I'd unleash my poison in full force.

"What, you don't believe me?" I'd say. "Why did you come all the way down here just to call me a liar?"

I'd make so much noise and cause so much drama that by the time my visitor left they'd be completely worn out. In this manner, I managed to carry on with my crystal meth addiction without anyone in my family finding out.

At the time, I thought that unleashing my poison made me strong. After all, it made the adults in my life do what I wanted. Nobody was in charge of me except me—and didn't that make me a man? It would be many years before I realized that attaining true adulthood means learning to control your poison. It is restraint, not reactivity, that makes us strong.

Controlling Your Poison

What does it mean to control your poison as skillfully as an adult rattlesnake? It means using your words with care, instead of lashing out in anger. It means telling the truth instead of lying, even when the truth will make you vulnerable. Most of all, it means refraining from the countless tricks that human beings play in an attempt to control the people around them when they feel emotionally threatened, whether that's playing the victim, laying on a guilt trip, creating drama and distraction, threatening to withdraw your love, or hundreds of other strategies.

When we feel threatened, it's normal to want to draw on any tools at our disposal to make the uncomfortable feeling go away. In many cases, we've even been domesticated by our parents or caregivers to lash out as hard as we can; very few of us were ever taught another way. Every person's poison is different, and learning to recognize your particular set of poisons can take time—let alone developing the courage to set them aside.

Controlling your poison doesn't mean repressing legitimate anger or allowing other people to walk all over you. In certain circumstances, expressing anger in a calm and respectful way really is the best thing to do. After all, the whole reason rattlesnakes have poison in the first place is to protect themselves from predators. Learning to distinguish the healthy and protective venom from the destructive kind becomes a lot easier when you can be honest with yourself and ask, *Am I setting a healthy boundary—or reacting in fear?*

As a teenager in Tijuana, I didn't yet know the difference between those things. But a shocking event would cause me to question the ways I'd been using my poison for the first time.

Exercise: Know Your Poison

The first step in controlling your poison is to *know* your poison. What are your go-to strategies for gaining control of a situation when you feel threatened?

Maybe you create a distraction by accusing the other person of wrongdoing; or you make a bid for sympathy by complaining about how hard your life is; or you simply shut down, refusing to say a word.

Write down a list of your strategies. Realize that these are all ways you have tried to feel safe.

Next, take a deep breath and sincerely thank yourself for these attempts at protection, no matter how crude they may be. Honor yourself for doing your best.

Finally, go through your list of strategies and cross them out one by one. As you do so, imagine that you are bidding them farewell. You are safe now; you don't need them anymore.

Exercise: Rattlesnake Meditation

Throughout the ages, shamans have connected with the consciousness of animals to gain access to their unique wisdom and way of viewing the world. In this exercise, I invite you to explore the wisdom of the rattlesnake.

First, sit in a comfortable position in a place where you won't be disturbed.

Next, imagine that you are a rattlesnake sensing a threat.

Feel yourself lifting your head, tasting the air, and bringing yourself into a striking position.

Allow yourself to see the threat—perhaps a hungry coyote. Feel the poison rising within you, and your jaws stretching wide.

Now, see the threat backing off. Maybe you even realize that it wasn't a threat at all—not a hungry coyote, but a curious and harmless puppy. Allow yourself to close your jaws and relax back down into the grass.

Notice how much energy you have, thanks to your restraint. Notice how good it feels to go on your way without harming or being harmed.

2

Shedding Skins

It is when we lose control that we repress the emotions, not when we are in control.
—don Miguel Ruiz

At seventeen, my best friend was JC Camacho, whom my friends and I nicknamed "Elmo" for his thick eyebrows and black hair. Everybody in our friend group loved Elmo because he was always happy. Most of us listened to Jane's Addiction and other rock bands, but Elmo was the first to get into techno music and start going to raves. When we hung out at my house, Elmo and I would have long, far-out conversations about music, our words trailing off into knowing laughter.

"Man, you know that feeling when you're at a concert and you catch somebody's eye and you just *know* you're feeling the same thing without even talking?" I'd say.

"Yeah, man! I know!" Elmo would reply.

All of our friends worked for the same moving company, and we saw each other every day. One day, someone in our group got a hold of an expensive bottle of whiskey. For the rest of our shift, we all felt so happy and excited that we would get to drink it at the end of the day. After work, we all went home, showered, and dressed up, as if for a big celebration. Then we met up again to enjoy this fancy whiskey together. My friend Gustavo, whose father owned the moving company, declared, "Today, we're going to drink like kings."

Elmo protested, "No, man! I don't like that at all! I don't want to pretend to drink like kings. Why don't we pretend that we're commoners who are walking around the kingdom and we find this amazing bottle, and we go into our little hut, and we drink it together."

We all thought it was so great that Elmo wanted to pretend to be exactly what we were, instead of pretending to be something we weren't. We spent the night drinking the whiskey and laughing together. None of us needed to pretend to be anything at all, because we loved and accepted each other.

A few weeks later, Elmo and some of our friends decided to take a trip to the beach to party. I really wanted to join them, but my father had insisted that I spend the weekend with him in San Diego. I was so bummed on the drive to California I barely said a word. I kept thinking about all the fun I was missing with my friends. I'm sure I wasn't much fun to be around that weekend, but my dad didn't seem to mind me sulking around the house. "Jose, go help your grandmother," he'd say, and of course I would comply.

When my dad dropped me off in Tijuana the next Monday morning, my friends Emilio and Daniela were hanging out on my front porch.

"Hey guys!" I said, smiling broadly. "How was the beach?"

Emilio and Daniela were quiet. One of the other kids said, "Did you hear what happened to Elmo?"

"Don't tell him," Emilio said.

But before Emilio could stop him, the kid said, "He got loaded and crashed his car. He's dead."

At first, my mind went blank. I couldn't comprehend that my funny, smart, talented friend was gone from this life forever. He would never drink another whiskey, make another joke, or go to another rave. We would never talk about music again. He was gone.

It was the first time in my life that a close friend my age had died. Before that moment, I thought death was something that happened to old people. It had never really occurred to me that *anyone* could die at any time. This realization frightened me. I knew that the accident could very easily have happened to me, or to any of us, because we all used drugs and drank alcohol and took senseless risks.

In the days and weeks that followed Elmo's death, I realized that I needed to change my life. I needed to stop using crystal meth and living in a filthy drug house. I needed to stop pushing my family away. After some deep soul-searching, I went to my father and told him about the destructive way I had been living—the drugs, the cravings, the endless quest to score my next high. With tears falling down his cheeks, he said, "Welcome back home, my son. Welcome back home."

Of course, I wasn't quite ready to stay home. I would need more painful lessons first.

Releasing Painful Habits

As humans, we all have moments of clarity when we recognize our own insanity and decide to make a change. In these moments, we begin the process of shedding our old skin and moving on. We vow to leave this old skin behind and start a new life. But for many of us, it's only a matter of time before we begin to feel uncomfortable. It's hard to live without our old skin. We're no longer sure who we are or where we belong. At least in the old skin, we knew! Forgetting our great vows, we go back to doing the very things we intended to change.

Many of us need to go through this cycle many times before we're truly ready to let go. We know we need to make a change, yet we keep on doing the same old thing over and over again. We're attached to the temporary release we get from our habit, even if it comes at a terrible cost. Instead of letting go, we hang on, dragging our old energy around with us.

Which brings me back to my good friend, the rattlesnake. Rattlesnakes shed their skins up to twelve times a year. In fact, baby rattlesnakes can shed their skins up to once a week—that's how fast they grow. When a rattlesnake is shedding, it's very vulnerable. Often, it withdraws to a safe place for a few days or a week—however long it takes to shed the old skin.

But when the rattlesnake is finished shedding, it goes on its way, leaving its old skin behind.

Can you imagine what it would be like if every time the rattlesnake shed its skin, it held on to it, carrying it everywhere it went? After a while, you wouldn't see the snake at all—you would only see the huge bundle of old skins it was carrying. Yet this is exactly what we tend to do as humans. We take our old experiences, good and bad, and we drag them with us everywhere we go. Imagine if we had the power to detach and start anew, with no preconceptions about who we are or what we are capable of.

At seventeen, I knew I had to detach from the old skins I was dragging around. In particular, I had to let go of my story as a victim of my parents' divorce, a self-image I used to justify my wild behavior and drug addiction. By clinging to this old skin, I was putting myself at risk of ending up just like Elmo—tragically losing my life at a young age, devastating my friends and family. I would also have to shed my story as a victim and derelict and learn to see myself as somebody worthy of love, good health, safety, and self-care.

Nobody could take this journey for me—not even my father, the shaman and healer don Miguel Ruiz. But at least by asking for help, I had taken the first step.

Exercise: Shedding Skins

A skin is like an identity we have created in our mind, and clinging to it after it's served its purpose prevents us from growing in a new direction. If you are struggling to shed a skin, it can be helpful to remind yourself of all the times in your life when you have already done this successfully. For example, maybe you left an unhealthy relationship, or gave up a job or pastime that used to define you.

Take out your journal and make a list of all the skins you've already shed. Include things like old jobs, past relationships, former habits, health conditions, and identities such as athlete, star student, perfect daughter, or drama queen.

How does it feel to realize that you've let go many times before? Does it make it easier to let go now?

Exercise: Clean Slate

Sometimes, stepping into a new story can be as easy as cleaning your room.

The simple act of cleaning is mentally energizing and emotionally uplifting, a powerful way of signaling to yourself that you are loved, valued, and deserving of a fresh start.

Choose a space in your home that represents the change you would like to make in your life. Then spend an hour cleaning the space, getting rid of any objects or visual reminders that link you to the habit you are trying to shed.

When you are done, take a moment to stand still and quietly state your intention for changing your life.

What does it feel like to walk into the refreshed space, now that you've made room for new possibilities?

3

The Illusion of Judgment

*Sometimes you have to get comfortable in
the uncomfortable until the uncomfortable
passes and you are comfortable again.*
—My grandfather, don Jose Luis Ruiz

When I told my father about my crystal meth addiction, he decided to send me to India to stay with my stepmother, Mama Gaya, and my stepbrother Rama Krishna. They lived at the ashram of Swami Kaleshwar, just outside the village of Shirdi. This was where the Indian saint Sai Baba of Shirdi had lived, and where thousands of devotees came every year to worship at the temple that had been built in his honor. Even though my father and Mama Gaya had separated the year before, I was still very close with her, and considered her my spiritual mother. Ever since I was a child, she'd been able to see right through me. She was like a clear mirror reflecting me back to myself, and I couldn't hide anything from her.

At the time I visited, Shirdi was a small village of perhaps twenty thousand people. Coming from Tijuana, a city of two million, I was shocked by how quiet it was—it reminded me of the tiny village in Jalisco, Mexico, where my grandmother grew up. In Shirdi, the Sai Baba temple was the main attraction. Other than that, there was a fruit and vegetable market, a few small hotels, a handful of small restaurants and lunch counters catering to devotees on pilgrimage, and a central plaza with benches and a beautiful fountain.

There was much to love about Shirdi. Instead of hanging out on the street corners drinking beer, like they did in Tijuana, people hung out drinking chai and eating cookies. Rama Krishna and I rescued orphaned puppies together. There was a sense of love and peacefulness permeating the village—but some days my mind was just too restless to enjoy it. I was glad that I'd brought my comic book collection with me—about three hundred in all.

I loved Mama Gaya and Rama Krishna, but it was also hard to adjust to the disciplined life of the ashram. The other students were all adults, and earnest spiritual seekers. Many of them were kind to me and enjoyed joking around with me and borrowing my comic books, but some saw me as a spoiled kid who was being given special treatment I didn't deserve. They frowned when I broke the ashram's rules or skipped meditation sessions. As for Swami Kaleshwar, he was a very disciplined teacher. He would have us meditate or sing *bhajans*, or devotional songs, for hours at a time, sitting on the hard marble floor without so much as a yoga mat to make ourselves comfortable. At night, all the students at the ashram would sleep on the floor—there were no private rooms or other luxuries. I didn't mind the physical discomfort, but I did miss the freedom and privacy that came from having my own place.

My initial relief at getting away from my drug addiction soon turned to restlessness, and after a couple weeks I was feeling homesick and desperate to go back to Tijuana. Life in a drug den was ugly, but life in an ashram was *hard*. I missed my friends, my music, and the familiar streets of my neighborhood.

To distract myself one day, I walked to the center of town and sat in the plaza. As I was sitting there, plotting a way to get myself back to Mexico, a couple of English-speaking businessmen walked up and stood nearby. They were chatting, and I was doing my best to understand their English, wondering what the big words meant, when a beautiful old man came into the center of the plaza. He was a vagabond I had seen wandering the village on a couple other occasions. He began dancing and singing bhajans very loudly while moving around the fountain, unaware and unconcerned that anyone was watching him.

One of the businessmen turned to the other and said, "Look at that old man. I think he's crazy."

The other man stood in silence for a few moments, watching the old man. He replied, "That man might be crazy, but he is in love with life. Are you in love with life?"

His colleague thought for a moment and then said reluctantly, "No."

"Then who's crazy?" was his companion's reply.

This stranger's wise words penetrated deep within my heart. I thought to myself, *Am I in love with life? Am I truly doing what I love to do?* At that point in my life, I had numbed myself completely with drugs and alcohol. I didn't even know who I was beyond the immense craving for my next high and the intense excitement of how I was going to score it—not to mention the strong paranoia of getting caught and incarcerated. I thought to myself, *I don't even know who I am.*

I got up from the bench, put my hand over my heart, and bowed deeply to the man who had seemed to speak directly to me. Then, with pure love, I bowed toward the beautiful vagabond who was still dancing and singing. Somehow, they had both reminded me why I had come to India in the first place—to fall in love with my life, instead of flirting with death. Elmo had died, but I was still alive. I still had a chance to shake off the chains of my addiction and choose a different path. Who cared if some of the other students at the ashram thought I was a brat? It was my life, not theirs. Their judgments had nothing to do with me.

Love Disarms Judgment

One of my favorite Buddhist stories tells of Siddhartha sitting peacefully under the Bodhi tree. A demon named Mara comes along and tries to shoot him with arrows. However, because of Siddhartha's immense love, the arrows turn into roses, falling harmlessly on the grass.

Mara's arrows are like the judgments of others, seeking a way to pierce our vulnerable hearts.

When you are living in a state of self-doubt and self-recrimination, it's very easy for these arrows to hurt you—after all, you've already done most of the work for them by hurting yourself. If you believe that you are a good-for-nothing brat, all Mara has to do is fire off an arrow in that direction and you will welcome it into the wound you created.

But if you truly love yourself, and believe only good things about yourself, those arrows have nowhere to go. Instead, they turn into roses. You realize that the demon who fired those arrows is the one who is actually hurting, not you. The more secure and unconditional your love is, the harder it is for others to cause you pain. Instead of getting angry at them for trying, you can see them as a vulnerable, fallible, hurting person; you know the pain they must be in to attack you in this way.

How do we cultivate this ability to turn arrows into roses? By falling madly in love with life, just like the "crazy" man in the town square. Falling in love with life means developing a deep appreciation for every aspect of existence, including the difficult ones. Of course, falling in love with life also means falling in love with yourself: with your body, which serves you so faithfully every day; with your breath, which connects you to so many other living beings; with your mind, with its powerful ability to create; and with your heart, with its capacity for forgiveness. It is by falling in love with yourself that you truly transform the arrows of others into roses, every time and every day.

As I settled into life at the ashram, I could tell that some of the people around me thought there was something off about me. But did I need to let their judgments define me? Or could I let those arrows turn to roses, and fall in love with my life?

Exercise: Removing Targets

When you have negative beliefs about yourself, you provide targets for the arrows of others. By dissolving these negative beliefs, you leave behind no target for those arrows to hit.

First, make a list of the negative beliefs you hold about yourself, whether they are obvious or subtle. For example, "I'm not good at music" or "I always mess up my friendships in the end."

Next, take a moment to reflect on where these beliefs came from. Are they the result of the domestication you received in childhood? Did you self-domesticate in an attempt to keep yourself safe after a traumatic experience?

Next, rewrite these negative beliefs as areas of potential growth. For example, "I have enormous potential for learning music" or "I am becoming a better friend every day."

Notice how these statements remain true no matter what your experience has been in the past.

Just like that, you have transformed your negative beliefs into positive beliefs brimming with potential. Instead of targets for arrows, you have a garden where roses can grow.

Exercise: Turning It Around

The next time someone judges you, can you turn it around by feeling compassion for them instead?

First, take a moment to identify what this person's wound might be. Since we are all mirrors for one another, it's often the case that we are suffering from what we accuse others of, and vice versa. For example, the person who calls you "crazy" for singing and dancing may be deeply repressing the joy and sensuality of their own life. The person who calls you a liar is likely living behind lies in their own life.

Allow yourself to imagine what it must be like for this person to live with this wound every day. Get a glimpse of the sadness, pain, and limitation they are living with, without overwhelming yourself.

Next, tune into the warmth and love of your own heart. Make a silent wish for this person to experience freedom, joy, and meaning.

Respond to the arrows they fire at you by giving roses in return.

4

Attention, Intention, Action

Wherever you put your attention,
this is what you will perceive.
—Barbara Emrys

A few weeks later, the students at the ashram all took a trip to Hampi, an ancient city on the Tungabhadra River that was famous for its ruins. We meditated in the river for several hours, then dried off and walked to a nearby field where many other tourists and travelers were milling about. Shortly after we'd gathered in the field, Swami Kaleshwar arrived, his beautiful white robes fluttering in the wind. One of the students said excitedly, "Watch, the swami is going to open a vortex for us!" For those of you unfamiliar with the term *vortex*, in this context it refers to an opening of an energetic connection to the divine, a bridge between the spiritual and material worlds.

Swami Kaleshwar joined us in the field and began to pray. All around me, the other students and many of the travelers began closing their eyes and lifting their arms in the air, opening their hearts to his teachings and words. I could tell that many of them were feeling a powerful energy, as if the swami's love and attention had awakened their own ability to love and be present. I also noticed one man standing in the circle with his arms crossed, watching intently with a slight frown. His skepticism was apparent. I could almost see a thought bubble over his head saying, *We'll see about this vortex!*

When the ceremony was finished, everyone spoke excitedly about their experiences. Many people reported seeing and feeling incredible things. In their view, Swami Kaleshwar had summoned a powerful energy field. They believed that he was capable of doing this, and so this is what they saw. When it came time for the reserved man to speak, he said, "I didn't see or feel anything." Because he was closed to the idea of the vortex, all he saw was a man in a white robe saying prayers in a field.

Observing the power of the students' belief in Swami Kaleshwar reminded me of a trip I took to the Mayan jungle with my father when I was eleven years old. At that age, I yearned to see a jaguar, and I kept begging him, "Papa, I want to see a jaguar. I want to see a jaguar." I repeated this request over and over again, giving full attention to my desire. After hearing my request multiple times, my father turned to me abruptly. With power in his words, he said, "If you really want to see a jaguar, Son, then you will see a jaguar." And he turned and walked away.

I continued to explore the jungle-filled ruins in Palenque. I scanned the jungle intently, remembering my father's words: *You will see a jaguar.* Suddenly, I saw a pair of bright blue eyes shining through the thick trees and plants, watching me with curiosity. We locked eyes for only a moment before the creature turned and flipped its tail toward me, bounding into the jungle. I saw its golden fur covered in dark spots and realized that I had just seen a young jaguar. Knowing that its mother couldn't be too far away, I felt a little frightened, and I ran back to the hotel as fast as I could to tell my father what I had seen.

We create our experience of life based on what we believe, what we intend, and where we place our attention. The audience members who *intended* to see the swami open a vortex, *believed* that he was capable of doing so, and paid *attention* to feelings and sensations that confirmed this belief were rewarded by an incredible experience; the man who did not set his intention, belief, or attention in this manner remained unmoved. Nobody in the field that day was "right" or "wrong" about the vortex—they simply had the experience they wanted and expected to have.

Opening the Vortex

When I think back on that day with Swami Kaleshwar, I believe that what some of the students called a "vortex" was simply the energy of their own love, belief, and concentration, which had been awakened and inspired by the swami's. We all open the vortex for ourselves when we open our hearts. Watching a guru or spiritual master can inspire us and give us an example, but it is our own intention and attention that determine what we experience—and our own actions that define our lives.

Many years ago, my father told me a story by the poet Homer. He said that the Greek gods were in the heavens speaking to one another. One of them said, "We only exist because the humans believe in us. When the humans stop believing in us, we will no longer exist." Putting your attention on something is the birth of that thought, idea, or dream. Once you intend to bring that thought into reality, that is the time to take action. Nurture the idea to make it grow into its full potential—give it your concentration and your belief. That's the real secret to opening a vortex.

The power of belief is evident at all levels of life. For example, our spiritual beliefs influence what we see, hear, and experience, sometimes in dramatic ways. Our belief in our own potential can influence whether or not we achieve our goals, or even pursue them in the first place. Our beliefs about health can determine whether we take proactive steps to nurture our well-being or throw up our hands and say, "It's all genetic, so why try?"

Modern medicine has shown the power of belief in the form of the placebo effect—a phenomenon in which certain patients recover upon being given sugar pills or other dummy treatments instead of pharmaceutically active medication. Thanks to a complex interplay between the patient's expectations of feeling better and their trust in the doctor, the patient's body begins to act as if the medicine is taking effect.

Knowing that our beliefs can be so powerful, it becomes especially important to take good care in noticing what we believe. When our beliefs are based on good science and verifiable facts, we can make responsible decisions for our health and well-being.

When our beliefs are rooted in ethics, we can take actions that benefit the many other beings with whom we share this beautiful planet. And when our beliefs about ourselves are saturated with love, we can grow into our full potential instead of caging ourselves with self-imposed limitations, and extend this love to others in whatever way it can be most helpful to them.

Being willing to update our beliefs is one of the keys to a life well lived. After all, science, archeology, physics, and other fields are providing new insights all the time. Now that we know the earth isn't flat, we can make better decisions about navigation. Now that we know the dangers of environmental pollution and climate change, we can take action that supports the health of the planet. And now that we know the incredible potential of human beings to be the artists of their own lives, there is no reason to dwell in negativity and shame.

When we tend to our beliefs about ourselves, others, and the world with care and intention, we give ourselves the palette we need to make a masterpiece of our lives. It is your belief that opens the vortex, so choose carefully which vortex you would like to see.

Exercise: The Power of Belief

The people around us play an important role in forming our beliefs, a process the Toltecs call *domestication*. Sometimes this domestication is positive, as when we are taught to believe that all humans deserve to live with dignity. Sometimes this domestication is negative, as when we are taught to believe that we are worthy only if we check off certain boxes of beauty, achievement, and wealth.

In this exercise, I invite you to notice how your basic beliefs were shaped, and by whom. To start, take out a pen and paper and create a few headings representing different realms of your life: for example, spirituality, romantic relationships, work, and money.

Next, write down how your beliefs about those aspects of life were formed, and by whom. For example, maybe your grandmother influenced your spiritual beliefs by teaching you to pray and your father influenced your beliefs about money by telling you to save every penny because you never know when you'll need it.

Next, take a moment to reflect on how these beliefs have shaped the artwork of your life. How have they affected your decisions? How have they propelled you forward or held you back? What kind of person would you be if you had been taught to believe the *opposite*?

Exercise: Vortex of Love

One of the most powerful beliefs you can hold is that you and everyone around you are deserving of unconditional love. When you have this belief, life becomes very beautiful, and very simple. You can open this vortex of love by starting each day with a simple ritual.

First, stand in a comfortable position with your feet hip distance apart.

Next, stretch your arms wide open, as if you're about to give the whole world a big hug. Imagine that all beings, including yourself, are contained within this loving embrace. Imagine peace and happiness sweeping over the whole world as all beings are touched by unconditional love.

Finally, wrap your arms around yourself and give yourself a big hug while vowing to keep this vortex open all day.

5

Being Given a Spiritual Name

*While we are here on this planet, we have
to do something noble with our lives.*
—Swami Kaleshwar

Slowly, I got used to life at the ashram. I learned
some bhajans that Sai Baba had written, and I
learned to meditate in the style Swami Kaleshwar
taught. I even began to feel some inner peace when
I meditated, as if the pain of my past was starting to
fade away. I was still skeptical and rebellious, but I
couldn't deny that an inner shift was taking place.

One day, I was at Mama Gaya's house when I
spotted an advance copy of my father's first book, *The
Four Agreements*, which had just arrived in the mail. I
picked it up and turned it over. On the back cover

there was a photograph of my father with his long hair and shaman hat, gazing into the mountains in Machu Picchu. As soon as I saw that photo, I felt a pang of longing. I said to myself, *Jose, it's time to go home.*

The week before I left India, Mama Gaya asked Swami Kaleshwar if he would give me a spiritual name. Swami was reluctant. He said, "You want me to give a name to the kid who reads comic books, skips meditation sessions, and cheats on the ashram's vegetarian diet to eat meat?" Mama Gaya just smiled and said, "Of course, only as you wish, Master Swami."

The day before I left, we went to the river and the swami had us meditate there all day. As I was bathing and meditating in the water, I gave silent thanks to India for all the eye-opening and life-changing moments. I thanked my father, Mama Gaya, and my stepbrother for their love, kindness, and patience. I thanked Swami Kaleshwar for all his teachings and his love. And I thanked the villagers in Shirdi who had shared tiny cups of chai, laughed, and petted puppies with me, and who made me feel like family.

That evening, as we sat together to eat my last meal at the ashram, Swami Kaleshwar called me to his seat at the head of the table. He asked if I had enjoyed my stay in India. I said, "Oh yes, Master. I enjoyed it very much. I am even wearing an 'I love India' T-shirt."

As I jokingly opened my jacket to reveal the T-shirt I was wearing, he laughed and asked, "Would you like to leave here with a spiritual name?"

I said, "As you wish, Master. I'm just grateful for all the teachings and love you have bestowed upon me."

He stood up and said, "With great honor, I would like to give you the name of Kaleshwar. I know you are not of this lineage, but I would like you to take my name. Go back to your lineage and incorporate the deep truths you've learned here into your own message."

With my hand over my heart, I bowed to my Indian master with deep gratitude and thanked him for the beautiful gift. As I was returning to my seat, some of the other students at the ashram began to voice their opinions.

"Hey, Swami, how could you give him your name? He doesn't come to class. And I saw him in town yesterday eating chicken."

"Yeah, Swami. He doesn't even practice the true Hindu teachings or do his chores in the ashram."

Swami put his hand up to stop the judgments. As the commotion quieted down, he said, "He may not practice the teachings completely, but he's pure of heart. He doesn't follow anyone just to be part of the group. He is skeptical of what people tell him, and he chooses only the teachings that serve him in his own beliefs and individuality. These are the traits that make a true master, and this is why he is worthy of my name."

The students listened to the Swami's words, but some of them weren't convinced; indeed, I could feel their resentment coming off of them like electricity. It wouldn't be the last time in my life that I would be scrutinized, criticized, or outright resented by people who thought I should be something different than what I was. Over and over again, I've seen people try to turn spirituality into a competition—or worse, a cult. They play games like "Who can get closest to the Master?" or "Which student is the most advanced?" Like children, they invent elaborate rules for these games and get very upset when people break them— just like when Swami Kaleshwar gave me his name. At a young age, I already understood that to follow my spiritual path, I would have to endure criticism and rejection from people who wanted to turn spirituality into this kind of game.

Following Your Own Path

Life isn't a competition, yet human beings find ways to create hierarchies all the same. We want to know which "level" we're on, as if we're playing a video game; we feel anxious or jealous if somebody else appears to be having special experiences or receiving special favors from the person in charge, whoever that happens to be. We try to get closer to the person at the top so that we can have a better chance of having those special experiences or accessing that special wisdom ourselves.

Yet all along, we have equal access to the nagual—the divine life force that lives within each person. No teacher or guru can give you more of this life force, and, for that matter, no teacher or guru can take it away. The nagual has been yours since birth and will be with you all your life.

Once you completely accept your own divine nature, spiritual practice becomes much easier. You realize that there's no need to follow the crowd—no need to pass every level and work your way to the top. Instead, you can follow your own path, appreciating life as it is instead of imagining all the incredible things that will happen when the teacher or guru decides you are ready. You can also stop worrying about being perfect, because as long as you're not holding yourself up as a pinnacle of spiritual achievement, others won't feel the need to judge and criticize you.

When Swami Kaleshwar gave me his name, it surprised the more "diligent" students at the ashram, but it surprised me even more. Maybe the way I was—rebellious, skeptical, fun-loving, bighearted, and a little self-deluded—wasn't bad. Maybe these were elements of spirituality, or at the very least, not mutually exclusive with spirituality. The swami's surprising gift showed me that while I was still lost in many ways, my heart was pointing me in the right direction.

Exercise: The Compass of the Heart

Think of a time when you followed your heart, even when it meant breaking the rules of your domestication.

For example, maybe you took a low-paying but meaningful job even though you'd been raised to value a high-paying career; or you spoke up against abuse even when it meant challenging a prominent person in your community.

As you reflect on this time, notice any pleasant sensations in your heart: for example, warmth, expansiveness, and calm.

The next time you feel the compass of your heart tugging you in a direction that breaks the rules, recall these positive feelings and let them guide you.

Exercise: Dropping Out of the Game

As children, many of us had the experience of getting fed up with a game that was too hard or unfair, putting our hands on our hips, and declaring, "I'm not playing anymore!"

In many cases, this refusal to keep playing is a good thing—we're asserting a healthy boundary around what we will and will not permit.

As adults, however, we sometimes forget that we're allowed to say, "I'm not playing!" Instead, we stay trapped in a game in which we're not having any fun or may even be getting hurt.

As you reflect on your life, can you identify any games you're tired of playing? For example, maybe you're playing emotional games with your spouse or partner, or competitive games with your coworkers or members of your spiritual community.

What would your life be like if you simply stopped playing? Notice any physical sensations that come up when you consider this possibility.

Finally, give yourself permission to say, "I'm not playing anymore," and walk away from this game.

6

Stepping into My Dream

How you treat yourself is how life will respond to you.
—Madre Sarita

After I got back from India, I spent the summer with my father in San Diego. At that point, *The Four Agreements* had been out for several months and he had been busy with book tours, presenting his teachings to large audiences across the United States. Prior to the release of *The Four Agreements*, my dad had been a fairly low-profile spiritual teacher who taught Toltec shamanism to a small group of apprentices. Then, seemingly overnight, he'd become famous, and it felt like everyone on the planet was reading his book.

Over the years, I'd always found an excuse not to go to my father's events. I was afraid that if I did, he would call me onto the stage without warning. I'd seen him put his apprentices on the spot over and over again, making them speak with no time to prepare. I had no doubt he would do the same thing to me if I ever gave him the chance.

One day, I was sitting comfortably in the living room, playing the latest version of *Super Mario Bros.* on my Nintendo, when my father walked in.

"I'm giving a talk today," he said. "You should come!"

No way, I thought. *I know exactly what you're gonna do if I come.*

As if reading my thoughts, he said, "Son, why don't you want to come to my lecture? Are you afraid I'm going to make you speak?"

"Yes, Papa," I said.

He smiled. "Don't worry, Son. You're not ready to speak in front of this big an audience."

I reluctantly agreed to go with him. At the conference center, I sat close to the front of the stage and watched as hundreds of people filed in. When my father spoke, I listened attentively and noticed the people around me responding to him with nods, smiles, laughter, and tears. My father's followers were educated people; judging from their clothes, many of them looked wealthy too. I was feeling so impressed and proud of my father, when he suddenly announced, "Now I would like to introduce to you my son."

Oh no, I thought. *Did I hear that right?*

I felt my legs weaken and my heart begin to pound. I stood up and slowly worked my way to the front of the conference center, hoping my older brother would magically appear so he could take my place. I walked up the stairs to the stage and stood next to my dad, gazing out at the sea of faces all looking right at me. The crowd was cheering. My father wrapped his arms around me, gave me a great big hug, handed me the microphone, and sat down.

My legs turned to jelly. I can't believe he's doing this to me, I thought. I'm a recovering addict—a junkie. What can I possibly have to say to all these normal, successful people?

I seriously considered saying, "Thank you so much" and hurrying off the stage. But then a memory came into my mind of standing in Madre Sarita's kitchen when I was ten years old.

"Jose, what do you want to be when you grow up?" she asked me.

"I want to do the same thing as you and Father," I said. "I want to be a Toltec teacher."

At the time, I didn't realize what I was asking for. Now, as the bright lights shone into my eyes, I realized that I was stepping into my childhood dream at last—whether I felt ready for it or not.

I began speaking into the microphone, addressing the audience in very broken English. I spoke from the heart, knowing that the people in the audience were probably only catching about half the words I was saying. At the same time, I understood that the content of my speech hardly mattered. What mattered was that I was finally summoning the courage to move beyond my fear.

When I stopped talking, the conference center filled with applause. People were smiling, reflecting the love in my heart back to me, even though they couldn't possibly have understood everything I was trying to say. Even though they didn't catch my words, they had caught my meaning. It was just like going to a rock concert, where you can feel the music deeply without ever knowing the lyrics to the song.

As I walked off the stage, I felt radiant and filled with purpose. Maybe, despite all that I had been through, I could still be a messenger of unconditional love. Maybe it wasn't too late to step into my childhood dream and follow in my father's and grandmother's footsteps as a teacher in our family's lineage. With a newfound lightness to my steps, I went to find my dad backstage and congratulate him on his event.

Finding Perfection Right Where You Are

Many of us think we need to be perfect before we can step into our dreams. We want to have all the pieces lined up so that nothing frightening or unexpected can happen; we want to eliminate all risk of embarrassment, struggle, or failure. If you had asked me when I would be "ready" to become a Toltec teacher, I would have said, "Once I've overcome all my demons and have my life figured out. Oh, and I'll need to be fluent in English, too." I certainly wouldn't have jumped on that stage as a shy teenager still processing a mountain of inner confusion and pain!

But life has a way of deciding when we're ready. We get thrust into the spotlight and handed the microphone, or an opportunity falls into our lap that we just can't pass up. At moments like these, the mind has a tendency to rebel. *I can't possibly do this. I'm not qualified at all.* Yet it is only by embracing those scary moments and leaping into the unknown that we discover our true potential. Often, we even discover that all the skills and resources we *thought* we needed to have before we stepped into our dream weren't as necessary as we thought; instead, all it takes is courage and an open heart.

In many cases, it's literally impossible to achieve a state of complete readiness. The classic example of this is having kids. No amount of studying or preparation can turn you into a parent; only *being a parent* can do that. The same thing is true of training a puppy, growing a garden, performing music, or teaching. You need to get your hands in the dirt long before you ever feel ready to do so. Not only that, but you need to give life the chance to be perfect, instead of expecting *yourself* to be. What looks to you like the wrong moment may be perfect from life's point of view, and it can take practice to drop your resistance and let that perfection be.

When my father called me up onto the stage in San Diego, I had to give up all my ideas about who I was and what I was and wasn't capable of. When those ideas fell away, all that was left was the nagual—and when I gave that nagual a voice, it spoke directly to the nagual living inside every member of the audience. It would still be a long time before I fully embodied the role of Toltec teacher, but I'd had my first glimpse, and by the warm feeling in my heart I knew that it wouldn't be my last.

Exercise: Dream Time

Often, the very things we believe make us unqualified to step into our dreams are treasures in disguise.

Think of a dream you hold dear—for example, starting a creative project or moving to a new town.

Next, write down all the reasons you're not ready to pursue this dream. Maybe you don't have enough money, the proper training, or the ideal state of health.

Now, write down all the reasons why this is in fact the ideal time to step into this dream. For example, maybe you're short on money, but you do have the energy and vigor to take advantage of all the job opportunities in your new town.

Going through your original list item by item, turn all the reasons you're not ready into reasons you are. When you can see things from a different perspective, you may discover that what you thought was holding you back can also propel you forward.

Exercise: Speaking from the Heart

Often, we hesitate to speak if we haven't planned out the perfect thing to say. Yet speaking from the heart can move people more than the most carefully planned delivery.

Every day for a week, make a point to speak from the heart to a friend, partner, or loved one. Don't rehearse or think about what you'll say; instead, open your heart and spend a minute telling them how much you love or appreciate them, or offer a simple wish for them to have a good day. It could be the same person or a different person every day. You could also leave a voice message if you can't reach them.

Notice how good it feels to share your love and appreciation with friends or loved ones even if you don't have anything "important" to say.

7

The Barrio Buddha

Stop going against yourself by sacrificing yourself. Listen to your own voice and have the courage to live by it, creating a beautiful atmosphere for the love of your life. Begin this by serving yourself with unconditional love.
—Mama Gaya

That summer, life at my dad's place was comfortable and predictable, full of teaching moments and spiritual conversations. India had had a profound effect on me, and even though I knew all the dangers of returning to Tijuana, something in me yearned to go back. I didn't quite feel at home in America. My English wasn't great, and I didn't know how to relate to my more "normal" and "successful" family members. I was also hiding a secret: I'd been sexually abused by a fellow drug user a few years earlier, and that experience made me feel like I was different from everyone else, permanently tied to an inner pain and shame. I thought that if I stayed in San Diego it was only a matter of time before the people around me figured it out. In Tijuana, it was easier to hide.

I told my dad I was ready to go back to Mexico. He gave me a long, searching look. "I trust you," he said.

I felt a prickle of self-consciousness. My father always knew when I was hiding things; still, he gave me space to make my own decisions and to follow my own path.

When I went back to Tijuana, my friends threw a big party to celebrate my return. A few hours into the party, a close friend of mine became very drunk. He came to me and said, "Jose, show us something. Your grandmother is a curandera, your father is a nagual, and you just returned from studying with a swami in India. Come on, show us something magical!"

I said, "Come on, dude, let's just have a good time." But, being drunk, he wouldn't take no for an answer. I gathered this group of kids, many of whom were involved in gangs and violence, and had them all sit down in lotus position on the concrete. I told them to close their eyes, and I began to share some of the teachings my father and grandmother had given me, as well as some teachings I'd learned in India. I finished by chanting some of the beautiful mantras that I had learned at the ashram. Pretty soon, an hour had passed. I told my friends to open their eyes, and they began talking about their experiences.

My drunk friend said to me, "Jose, what did you do to me? I'm not drunk anymore." I laughed and assured him that I hadn't done anything to him. He had been meditating for over an hour and had been able to clear his mind—not to mention that enough time had passed for the alcohol level in his bloodstream to drop.

Every weekend after that, when my friends would throw a party, they gave me an hour to speak to them and bring them into that place of meditation and peace. The beautiful thing was that when the neighborhood was experiencing gang-related conflict and violence, they would all protect me and send me home so that I would be safe. They called me the Barrio Buddha.

I began to meditate and sing bhajans for many hours every day. I hadn't become a Hindu follower, and yet I felt that Sai Baba's energy was helping me. But all my meditation couldn't keep me safe from crystal meth. Although I'd been clean for months, it was just too hard to say no when my friends were all passing a pipe around. Within a few months I had started using again, and shortly after that I was back in the familiar cycle of searching for drugs, using them up, and searching again.

One day when I went out to score a fix, another man threatened me and forced me into sexual acts. It was awful to see myself through that man's eyes:

as a stupid junkie, barely human, who could be used and thrown away like trash. I knew I was lucky he hadn't killed me, but at the same time the shame I felt was so unbearable, I almost wished that he had. This was the second time in my years of drug use that I'd been sexually assaulted, and the fact that it had happened twice seemed to mark me as a victim. Looking back, I realize that there's no way I was the only one of my friends to experience sexual violence from the dangerous men we interacted with, but at the time I believed I was alone.

All the progress I'd made in India and San Diego seemed to go down the drain. I was filled with so much fear and shame, all I could think about was getting my next high to escape it for a while. I didn't want anyone to touch me, and it was hard for me to be around my friends, especially the macho ones, because of the way they talked, making homophobic jokes and comments. I was afraid they would find out what had happened to me—that they would call me a *maricón*, a fairy, and cast me out of the group.

At the same time, I was filled with self-judgment. A real man would never have let this happen to him. What was wrong with me?

Before, the crystal meth had given me a fun, creative high; now it took on a darker character. My need for the drug grew intense and relentless. I began hanging out with hardened gang members and longtime drug users who were older than me. My old group of friends were afraid of them. "Jose," they would say, "how can you hang out with those people? Those are some real bad dudes."

My new "friends" would come to my house to smoke meth, then pass out on the floor. In exchange for staying at my house, they would share their drugs with me. Unlike my childhood friends, these new "friends" didn't truly care about me, or each other. At the first sign of trouble, they would disappear.

I began to isolate myself in my house, going out only when I absolutely needed to. Now and then, my father would come down from San Diego to see me. He'd been having nightmares about me, and he knew that something was wrong. But when he knocked on the door, I pretended not to be home. Once, he knocked for two hours and I just stayed in my room, determined not to let him see me in that state.

One day, my old friend Emilio came to see me. As we sat on my porch smoking a joint together, I told him about being sexually assaulted. He looked around at the filthy house, and at my face, which was skinny and hollow.

"You know, *gallo*, if you stay here, you're gonna die," he said. "You're already dead in life. You're not even living—you're not even here."

The Power of Words

I'll always be grateful to Emilio for speaking those words of truth to me when I needed them most. Words are powerful, and he used the power of his words to help me save my own life. Unlike the man who had hurt me, Emilio believed that my life had dignity and worth, and through his kindness, he helped me to believe that too. When a friend speaks truth to you, it's like looking in a mirror: suddenly, you can see the situation clearly, and there's no hiding anymore. But it takes trust to be able to hear those words and let them in.

How can we build that trust—the kind of trust that gives another person the chance to save our life? The kind of trust that lets us hear what another person is really saying, instead of dismissing it or brushing it off? It starts with believing that you are worthy of being helped. No matter what kind of self-destructive path you have been on, there is always a part of you that wants to live—a tiny seed that wants to grow and thrive. And no matter how many negative thoughts you have in your mind, this tiny seed knows its own worth.

When Emilio spoke those words to me, that seed woke up. I knew that he was right. I didn't want to put these substances into my body anymore. I didn't want to live in this hell. I would go back to California, leaving the old neighborhood for good, and leave my crystal meth addiction behind me. It was time for the Barrio Buddha to abandon the underworld ashram and walk into my family's loving embrace.

Exercise: Words of Wisdom

Think of a time when a friend or loved one told you the truth in a powerful way. How did their words of wisdom change your life? Write a letter, text message, or e-mail to this person letting them know the impact they had on you, even if the incident took place years or decades ago.

Exercise: The Beating Heart

Think of an experience or memory that brings up feelings of shame. Maybe you were abused, or you did something that you now regret.

Next, imagine the millions of people living on the planet right now who have been through a similar experience.

Imagine their hearts beating and their lungs breathing, all working hard to keep them alive.

Now, imagine your heartbeat and your breath joining with theirs, creating a powerful alliance of healing.

Realize that you don't have to heal alone, and neither do they—you are all healing together.

Return to this powerful state of collective healing whenever you need courage and strength.

8

Crossing the Border

*Kindness is the light that dissolves all walls
between souls, families, and nations.*
—Paramahansa Yogananda

I went back to San Diego and moved in with my
father and grandmother, this time for good. My
dad's place was a social hub, always filled with relatives coming and going. He was constantly teaching me without even saying a word. Just one look
from him, and I would see myself reflected clearly. I
would see whether I was fooling myself, whether I
was going against myself, and that awareness, painful though it sometimes was, helped me to heal.
As for Madre Sarita, she was a curandera who saw
her clients and patients at the house. I soon became

her assistant, a job that kept me busy and provided a much-needed distraction. Slowly but surely, I began to recover my sense of self-worth, and to treat myself with love instead of hurting myself.

Still, withdrawing from crystal meth wasn't easy, and I was trying to do it on my own, cold-turkey, and while keeping all my thoughts and emotions about it inside myself. The only thing that really helped with the cravings was cannabis, which calmed me down enough to ride them out. When the anxiety and jitters got too intense, I could sit out back with a joint, take some deep breaths, and slowly return to a sense of calm. Cannabis truly felt like a medicine to me, helping my battered nervous system recover from all the chaos I had put it through, although I now know I was simply changing one drug for another, perhaps less destructive one, and still avoiding the real healing and inner work that I needed to do.

To make matters worse, I didn't have a reliable source for cannabis in San Diego, so I soon ran out.

I decided to take a trip to Tijuana, where I could buy some easily from a dealer I knew. I told myself that buying some cannabis in Mexico was the responsible thing to do to make sure I didn't relapse on meth.

For some reason, I asked my mother and maternal grandmother if they would like to go to Tijuana with me. They agreed, and once we were past the border into Mexico, I dropped them off at the mall. Then I went to see my dealer and scored a couple joints, which I wrapped in plastic and hid in my pants. I knew they would help me get through the coming week, and I felt good knowing I was protecting my family from the reality of the terrible withdrawal symptoms I was experiencing. After walking around the neighborhood for a few hours, I went to pick up my mom and grandma from the mall.

As we waited in the long line of cars to cross the border back into the United States, I heard drug detection dogs going from car to car. I only had a couple joints on me, so I naively thought the dogs wouldn't be able to smell them. But the dogs came up to our car and started barking like crazy. A pair of border patrol agents walked over and made us all get out of the car. They detained all three of us and impounded our car. I willingly gave the border patrol agents what I had stashed and told them I was solely responsible.

"Please let my mom and grandma go," I said. "They had nothing to do with this."

I saw fear and confusion in my poor grandmother's eyes and heard my mother crying. "I never thought this would happen to me," she said. A thick wave of guilt flowed through me. It kept on coming, like tar filling up a pothole.

After a few hours, the border patrol finally released my mother and grandmother. I was relieved as I watched them leave, but the guilt remained. My whole reason for buying cannabis was to help me stay off crystal meth; I was trying so hard *not* to go back into that hole and drag my family with me. But in my attempt to protect my family from my addiction, I'd managed to get them into trouble anyway.

The border patrol kept me detained for more than ten hours, which felt like ten days. I worried about my mother and grandmother and wondered if they were able to find a ride home. The border patrol questioned me over and over again, but because it was my first offense in the United States, they finally let me go. I paid a large sum of money to get my car out of impoundment, and I headed home to face the truth—the truth of my intense guilt, the truth of my lies, and the truth of the destructive mask I was still wearing.

I had crossed a border from the underworld to the world of the living, but I still had more work to do on myself. All my survival skills pertained to the *old* world—the world of dealers and drug users. I was used to being secretive and self-sufficient, and to justifying my actions and accepting the "lesser of two evils" rather than facing the truth. Now, I would need to learn how to be open and how to ask for help. I was realizing that shedding my "junkie" skin meant more than just giving up crystal meth and the marijuana I was using as a substitute. This skin was also made up of habits and character traits I'd mistaken for "me"—and now it was time to let them go.

New Life, Old Habits

As humans, we are very good at developing the skills we need to survive in any given situation. But when that situation changes suddenly, we can find ourselves clinging to our old tools, not realizing that new ones are needed. If you're an expert at deceiving others, you may be reluctant to start telling the truth, even when it's safe and easy to do so; if you've relied on self-sufficiency your whole life, you may hesitate to embrace the support of a community, even when that support is being offered to you wholeheartedly.

In many cases, we cling to our old ways of living even when it's clear that it no longer makes sense to. "I don't want to give up my tools!" we say. "I worked so hard to master them, and I don't know who I'd be without them." We fear that we will no longer be ourselves if we learn to live in a new way. We prefer the comfort of the known, even when we can see it is no longer serving us. In some cases, we're more attached to our survival skills and coping mechanisms than we are to our homes, relationships, or jobs!

In the Toltec tradition we often say that there is nothing to learn except how to *unlearn*. As human beings, we're awfully good at accruing layers to our identity, but it takes practice for us to let them go. Learning how to *unlearn* the habits that no longer serve us requires stepping into the present moment, instead of living in the past. It requires looking at the world through fresh eyes, being curious, and asking questions like "What's really necessary?" and "Which possibilities are open to me today that weren't open to me before?" If I had gone to my family and told them how badly I was suffering from my meth withdrawal, they could have helped me find support. Instead, I took matters into my own hands because doing things on my own was my survival strategy—and it almost got my mom and grandmother into deep trouble.

I knew that if I was going to stay drug-free and start a new life, there was a whole lot that I would have to unlearn—and I was just getting started.

Exercise: Beginner's Mind

The practice of meditation can give you access to what some Buddhists call beginner's mind—a wide-open state in which you can see the world through new eyes, unencumbered by what you think you know.

The next time you find yourself facing a problem, take ten minutes to meditate instead of jumping to solve it using the same old tools you always use.

Sit in a comfortable position and feel deeply into your body's sensations. Notice if your muscles want to spring into action, or your mind wants to rehearse possible things to say or do.

Let yourself simply *be* without being drawn into one of these familiar patterns. Watch them, feel them, but don't immediately follow their directives. This is a simple yet powerful practice to break old patterns and become open to other possibilities.

At the end of your ten-minute meditation, does your mind feel more open to new courses of action you haven't considered before?

Exercise: Unlearning

Think of a coping skill or survival strategy you no longer wish to rely on—for example, leaving events early so you don't have to mingle, or staying late after work just so you don't have to ask anyone for help.

First, take a moment to honor and appreciate all the ways this survival strategy has truly helped you in the past. Chances are, this strategy really did keep you safe from a threat at least once or twice, if not many times.

Next, address this part of yourself with love, gently inviting it to take a rest from protecting you in this way. For example, you might say, "Thank you so much for teaching me to be so capable and self-sufficient when there was nobody around to help me. But right now, I *do* have people to help me, so you no longer need to do this job."

By extending respect and gratitude to your survival strategies, you can dissolve them with ease instead of creating a battle within yourself.

9

A Trip to Egypt

Trust in the wisdom of your heart. It knows the way, even when the mind is clouded by doubt or confusion.
—don Miguel Ruiz Jr.

When I arrived home from the border incident, my father was waiting for me. He was holding a plane ticket to Egypt with my name on it, departing the following week. He didn't say much about what had happened, but spending two weeks in Egypt with him on one of his spiritual journeys was punishment enough to me. His teachings at that time were very intense, and a part of me, through my actions, was still rebelling against them. But instead of trying to get out of the trip to Egypt, I decided to count my blessings. I took the ticket and thanked my father for allowing me to participate.

This was back in the days when planes still had smoking and non smoking sections. I had been seated in the smoking section, and as the long flight wore on, more and more people from the non-smoking section strolled to the back of the plane to have a cigarette. They milled around, their bodies crushed up against the seats, their cigarette smoke filling the air. I got up and found a seat in the non-smoking section just to get away from all the commotion. The seat I chose was next to a woman named Lynn, who was a student of my father's. She was nineteen years older than me, a beautiful woman with brown hair, green eyes, and pale skin. When I sat down beside her, she recognized me as my father's son right away.

At that time in my life, I was very shy and withdrawn, especially when it came to women. To avoid speaking with anyone, I was wearing a large pair of sunglasses that covered nearly half my face. The first thing Lynn did was lift my sunglasses and look into my eyes. She said, "Your eyes are just like your father's, and that makes me love you." We talked for a while, and she told me about her marriage to an abusive man and how she had been saved by my father and his teachings. When all the passengers who had gone to the smoking section started migrating back to their seats, I stood up. Lynn said, "One thing I do know about myself is that I will never get married again." As I walked back to my seat, I thought, *I'm going to change that woman's mind.*

Lynn and I spent every moment in Egypt together. Falling in love seemed like the perfect solution to my out-of-control existence. *She* could take charge, and I could set down all the burdens of life. Like many victims of sexual abuse, I felt safer being with an older woman, who felt more like a mother than a sexual threat. I wouldn't have to make any decisions; I could just let her take care of me. And Lynn seemed perfectly content to do exactly that. In my view, she adopted me the way you'd adopt a puppy, happy to fuss over me and give me attention. She was a little embarrassed about having a relationship with a much younger man, but I was thrilled and wanted everyone to know.

Up until that point, I'd been a virgin. My only other girlfriend had been a quiet girl from my old neighborhood named Anna. I had adored Anna, but I'd left her because I didn't want to drag her into the world I was creating for myself through my drug addiction. Lynn and I made love for the first time while cruising down the Nile River. With this newfound pleasure, my love for Lynn grew even stronger. Although my father's other apprentices whispered about the age gap, I was certain I'd found my ticket out of the darkness at last. As for my father, he supported me just as he always had, but he also warned me about the red flags he saw in the relationship—mainly that I had lots of inner work I still needed to do and forming a healthy relationship wouldn't be possible until I had done so, but I was unable to hear the warnings.

When we returned to California, Madre Sarita expressed intense disapproval of our relationship. Her deepest wish was for me to have children, and she knew that Lynn was unlikely to have children with me at her age. Lynn was also a very wealthy woman who came from a well-known family, and my grandmother worried that I was just a passing fancy for her. She sternly informed Lynn that if she was going to be with me, she needed to marry me. She also told Lynn that I was just a child and that Lynn needed to take care of me. Lynn, having great respect for my family and my grandmother, did just that. We were married the following February.

I moved to Lynn's home in a fancy neighborhood in Malibu. I was excited to be in a new home, but also felt out of place among the wealthy white residents. The only people who looked and sounded like me were servants—cleaning pools, washing windows, and so on. At lunchtime, I would walk down to a construction site where a taco truck pulled up every day to feed the hungry workers. I'd buy some tacos that reminded me of home and chat with the workers in Spanish. When I told them I lived in the neighborhood, they thought I was joking. "You're kidding, *amigo*—now tell us where you work!" they said.

Thanks to the years I'd spent working for a moving company as a teen, I was in the habit of being of service. Whether it was cleaning up a mess, carrying boxes, or washing the moving truck, I would do whatever my boss told me to do. When I moved in with Lynn, I put myself at her service, taking on tasks as if I was her employee rather than her equal. I placed myself below her, and in this way the *paisanos* at the taco truck weren't totally wrong when they asked me where I worked—I just didn't punch a timecard for my job.

Still, in those early days, I felt that my marriage to Lynn was great. I was sober for the first several months of our marriage and felt proud of the way I'd changed my life. Lynn and I would go out for dinner at fancy restaurants, and I got to meet artists and intellectuals I never would have met in my former world. Her home was like an art museum, filled with paintings and sculptures, and I soon began collecting guitars, which are an art form in their own right.

But soon, our unmet expectations of one another began to make themselves known. I wanted a mother who would take care of me; she wanted a hero who would take away her pain. Because I was unwilling to address the underlying issues, it wasn't long before I began to drink again, and the ideal relationship that was supposed to change both of our lives turned into one of manipulation and pain. The truth is that we were both addicted to suffering, and instead of healing that addiction for one another, we spurred each other on.

The abuse we had both experienced throughout our lives—both from others and from ourselves—was magnified in our attempt to form a loving relationship. Because I didn't love myself, I had nothing to give to her. What I did have to give was blame, recrimination, and shame. And those things came flowing out in full force. While there were still moments of love, those moments were becoming fewer and further between. I struggled with intimacy and found it hard to be close to Lynn, either physically or emotionally.

Then I found out that Lynn had gone to my father and told him about the sexual assaults I'd experienced as a teen. I felt humiliated and betrayed. How dare she tell my father this sensitive secret? I'd confided in her. Before long, my father's apprentices were gossiping about me and my crazy life, using it to cast doubt on my father's teachings and vie for power among themselves. It was hard to watch so many "spiritual" seekers abandon true spirituality and follow their egos instead. And it was hard to feel that I couldn't trust my wife with my deepest secrets.

I had formed my ideas about what a relationship was supposed to look like by watching soap operas and listening to the chatter of the women in my life. When I thought about ending my marriage, those voices formed a chorus of resistance: "You should never cheat on your wife or divorce her." "Marriage is forever, and you should stay with one woman." "You should never be like your dad." If I ever expressed thoughts of leaving, Lynn would cry, and guilt would set in. I truly wanted to be the hero and the hopeless romantic who loved the same woman until death did us part. But how could I love her when I didn't even know how to love myself?

We'd been living together for six months when I began overeating and my drinking escalated further. Eating was one of the ways I found pleasure, and drinking was an escape. I gained a lot of weight. I was very unhappy and unsatisfied with who I was and what I had become. Just as I had seen some of my father's students try to misuse shamanism as a means of skipping past their inner wounds, I had hoped that my marriage would fix me and I could avoid my problems, and that somehow it would save me from looking deep inside at the raw, tender, and painful places within. Instead, I formed a little hole where I kept on worshiping the skeletons of my past, all the while using my idea of love to justify it.

Addiction to Suffering

Human beings have a special genius for finding drama, unhappiness, and turmoil wherever we go. No sooner do we solve one problem in our lives than we find another to obsess over—whether it's our "crazy" neighbor, our unreasonable boss, or our bank account which never has quite enough money. Our unhappiness is like a hermit crab, finding one new home for itself after another. All the different shells the crab inhabits for a while *look* different, but it's the same crab living inside each one!

Yet even the most intelligent people can go an entire lifetime without realizing what's going on. We truly believe that the external forms of our problems are making us unhappy, not realizing that the *real* problem is the addiction to suffering itself. Even when our lives are going well, we find reasons to blame, gossip, worry, and play the victim, just to get our fix of suffering and feel "normal" again. How much happier we could be if we realized that our addiction to mental suffering is the real problem. Then, we could train our minds to break the habit of seeking out suffering and enjoy the peace and calm that is all around us.

My own addiction to suffering was fed by a deep belief in my victimhood. Nothing was ever my fault or my responsibility; everything bad that happened to me was due to my parents' divorce or some other event beyond my control. If I was no longer the victim of crystal meth, I could now be my wife's victim—and it didn't even require her consent. I believed I needed to be hurting all the time, and so I used whatever was within reach to hurt myself; it didn't matter if it was crystal meth or marriage.

It would be years before I stopped martyring and abusing myself in the name of love—and before I saw my addiction to suffering for what it really was.

Exercise: Stalking Suffering

The Toltec tradition teaches that we can stalk our own minds the way a skillful hunter stalks his or her prey. By stalking our own minds, we can discover the subtle patterns that might not have been apparent to us before.

Carry a pen and small notebook around for one day.

Every time you notice your mind generating suffering about something, jot down the general category. For example, "money" or "relationship with Mom."

At the end of the day, review your list. Which aspects of life cause you the most suffering? Are you surprised by how many times a day you're pouring mental energy into these areas of your life?

Exercise: Releasing Suffering

Look at your list from the previous exercise.

For the next week, set aside ten minutes a day to *intentionally* suffer about these problems. During those ten minutes, suffer about them as much as possible. Let your imagination run wild. Notice if it gets harder to suffer when you bring this activity into your conscious awareness.

Then, any other time you catch yourself suffering, remind yourself that you have your ten minutes set aside that day already, and try to drop or ignore the suffering thoughts. It's helpful, but not always easy, to turn your attention to something else. Can your mind find something positive to think about in that moment instead? There is always peace and beauty in the present moment; bring your attention to that.

If you like this practice, stick with it past a week, gradually scaling back or eliminating the number of minutes you designate to suffering, but continue with the training of your mind to find the peace and beauty that always exists, remembering that suffering is an addiction you are letting go of.

10

Heavy Metal

Truth is exact correspondence with reality.
—Paramahansa Yogananda

Even as my marriage to Lynn was filled with an addiction to suffering, there were still some bright spots during this period in my life. For one thing, living in Los Angeles meant I could see my favorite rock and metal bands on a regular basis. Standing in a crush of people, the music roaring in my ears, I could forget my troubles and connect to something bigger than myself.

One day, a friend asked me to take him to my favorite place to meditate.

"Sure!" I said. "I'm going to an Iron Maiden concert tonight. I'll take you along."

"Jose, be serious," he said. "I mean someplace quiet, like a garden or temple."

"I *am* serious," I said. "Just wait, you'll see."

At the stadium where the concert was being held, I closed my eyes and swayed along to the music, feeling the incredible vibrations of the electric guitars, the passion in the singers' growls and roars, and the energy of the other fans. Soon, a sense of deep peace and unity came over me as I lost myself in the sound. Meanwhile, my friend watched me, perplexed. He couldn't feel the peace I was feeling.

"Jose, there's no way I can meditate in such a loud and crowded environment," he groaned. "I'm going home."

My friend wasn't wrong, and neither was I; we just had different ways of getting to that place of peace and light. Although by that point in my life I'd done countless hours of silent meditation, sitting alone on a cushion or among hundreds in an ashram, there was nothing that could transport me to a state of stillness like a heavy metal concert. In fact, I'd once surprised a Tibetan singing bowl master by telling her that the sound healing she'd given me reminded me of an Ozzy Osbourne concert— and that's why I loved it so much!

I hear mantras in the thick guitar chords— *ommms* hidden deep within lyrics like "Mama, I'm coming home." When the fans in the audience start singing along, it feels like the whole stadium is an ashram, *ommm*ing along with a sincerity and earnestness that touches my soul. And while heavy metal fans may *look* different from the spiritual seekers at an ashram, they are often engaged in a very similar process of shedding the self and merging with the divine.

Mama Gaya Returns

Another bright spot during this time was when my stepmother, Mama Gaya, came back from India. She visited me in Los Angeles and encouraged me to step into the spiritual gifts I'd received at Swami Kaleshwar's ashram. She gave me some white robes to wear, and a beautiful orange robe she had sewn for me out of silk. I began to wear them wherever I went, not only to recognized places of worship like Paramahansa Yogananda's Self-Realization Fellowship Temple in Santa Monica, or the Ramakrishna temple in Santa Barbara (both of which I visited frequently) but also on my everyday errands around town.

One day, I took a trip to a large spiritual bookstore, a popular meeting place for the New Age community. My long black hair was neatly gathered in a ponytail, and I was wearing my white robes. As I browsed the bookshelves, many people came up to me and asked me questions about life, assuming I was some kind of guru or monk. They asked me about spirituality and the Indian tradition. They were all kind and attentive and showed great respect for the teachings I had to offer.

Just a few days later, I went back to the same neighborhood in Los Angeles. However, I had attended a heavy metal concert the night before, and I still had on my black leather pants, a black leather jacket, and a black concert T-shirt. My tall black boots were wrapped in metal spikes, and my hair was snarled and falling down over my shoulders. I walked past the same spiritual bookstore and decided to go inside.

I strolled in and started looking around. This time, the people at the bookstore didn't flock to me the way they had a few days before. In fact, the only person who showed an interest in me was the security guard, who began following me around the aisles. The other shoppers shot me disapproving looks, and I felt so uncomfortable that I left, making a mental note: *Appearances* do *matter.*

What happened? I was the same person on the inside; I had felt the same spiritual feelings at the metal concert the night before as I had at the ashram in India. Yet the people at the bookstore assumed I was a good-for-nothing metalhead who couldn't possibly have a legitimate reason for being there. I realized that if I had worn my white robes to the concert the night before, something similar might have happened. The metalheads may have assumed I was a good-for-nothing New Ager who couldn't possibly have a legitimate reason for being at the concert!

While my experience at the bookstore was disappointing, I thought it was hilarious that people could be so easily fooled by my appearance—that they would assume I had deep spiritual knowledge based on the costume I was wearing and treat me with outsized respect, only to treat me with disrespect the moment that costume came off. In that moment, I vowed to myself that I would always respect everyone, whether their religion was Hinduism or heavy metal.

Everything Is Spiritual

The truth is that everything becomes spiritual when we give it our love and attention. Heavy metal may sound like noise to a person who doesn't love it— but to the heavy metal devotee, those deep hums, growls, and screams are the sound of God or Source or a higher power. Likewise, silent meditation on a cushion may feel like the peak of boredom for some of us, while others relish the tranquility of quietly counting their breaths. There is no right or wrong way to meditate, and there is no right or wrong way to find your own inner peace, your spirituality. *Everything* is spiritual in its own unique way.

Today, there is a big war surrounding spirituality. Of course, this is just a war of belief systems. It plays out all around us, but especially in the world of social media. There, it is easy to forget that a complex human is represented in a digital image and words, and we reduce them to an idea we stand against. But this war has been around for a lot longer than modern technology. We can find the same war of beliefs in ashrams, churches, and meditation centers, and in workshops and on retreats.

Sometimes, the warring beliefs take the form of subtle judgments; other times, people's differences can erupt in violent dramas. Instead of supporting others in their spiritual paths, we create hierarchies, and these distract us from what's really important — the practice of unconditional love for ourselves and others.

Ever since that day in the bookstore, respect has remained central to my spiritual practice. The word *respect* comes from the Latin word *respectus*, which means "to look back" or to look at something in detail. I find this very telling. When we give something our respect, we do not glance at it briefly, dismissing it out of hand, but rather pause, look again, and allow ourselves to see it deeply. If anyone at the spiritual bookstore had taken a look back and seen the sincerity in my eyes, they would have realized that I was just as pure of heart as I was when I wore my Hindu robes. The quality of our looking is the quality of our respect.

When we take the time to see others clearly, our natural respect for them increases. Of course, the same is true when we bring that quality of looking to ourselves. How often do we disrespect ourselves, dwelling on perceived imperfections while failing to see the divinity within? How often do we question our own paths, scolding ourselves for loving what we love or practicing how we practice? How often do we look at others, wishing we could be more like them? By looking back at ourselves with love, we can learn to respect our own paths and appreciate the grace that was present all along.

Exercise: Respect as a Practice

When I travel, I like to stop at sacred places and show my respect—whether it's at a Catholic cathedral, an Indian ashram, or a burial mound in the mountains of Peru. In this exercise, I invite you to cultivate respect for traditions that might be unfamiliar to you.

The next time you're away from home, make a point of visiting a sacred site from a different tradition.

Walk around the grounds; appreciate any artwork or carvings you see.

If possible, sit in silence for a few minutes and try to feel the qualities that make this place important to people.

Can you feel a sense of peace and respect here even if you are unfamiliar with the specifics of the tradition?

Exercise: Looking Back

If you have dismissed someone's spiritual practice in the past, I invite you to look back with curiosity and respect.

Make a point of asking that person about their practice and what it means to them.

If possible, join them for a few minutes of practice, a lecture, or a special event like a ritual or ceremony in their tradition.

Can you get a glimpse of the meaning they find in this practice when you bring the quality of respect to your looking?

11

Welcoming Home
the Love of My Life

Three things cannot hide for long:
the moon, the sun, and the truth.
—Buddha

One day, just a few months after Lynn and I had gotten married, I went to the dentist for a root canal. It should have been a routine procedure; but due to my former meth use, there was a complication and the anesthesia the dentist injected caused massive swelling between my eyes and my brain. Before I knew it, I was lying in a hospital bed, blind, while doctors discussed the best way to save my eyesight and protect my brain from permanent damage.

As I lay in the hospital bed, scared of what could happen, my thoughts seemed to be spinning out of control. *This never would have happened if you hadn't used crystal meth*, I scolded myself. *You're such an idiot! You deserve to be blind.* I began to panic as I contemplated all the beautiful sights I might never enjoy again: the sparkling ocean, the beautiful sunsets, the faces of my friends and family. What would I do if I couldn't drive anymore? How would I go to heavy metal concerts? Would my family have to take care of me for the rest of my life?

The moment one worried thought or self-criticism had completed itself, another one sprang up in its place, like fast-growing vines in the jungle. *Haven't you already been enough of a burden on your family? And now they have to deal with this!* Meanwhile, my mom and aunts hovered around my bed, crying and praying for me to be okay. When I heard their voices and felt their loving hands touch my arms and face, all I could feel was guilt and shame for causing them so much distress.

For the next five days, I was completely blind. Confined to a hospital bed without my usual distractions, I had a lot of time to observe my thoughts. At the same time, my senses of hearing, taste, and touch became heightened, and I discovered new dimensions of pleasure in a cup of coffee or the sound of a loved one's voice. Slowly, I surrendered to this strange new reality and even made a sort of peace with it.

On the fifth night of my hospitalization, I fell into a deep and restful sleep. I dreamt that Lynn and I were in the desert, walking hand in hand toward a cave. As we got closer, I saw that there was a line of souls waiting to go in. I had a feeling that whatever was in that cave was not what the souls really needed. I told Lynn to take the souls and help them fly to the sun while I went to see what was inside.

The entrance to the cave was dark and cold. As soon as I'd stepped inside, a demon appeared. His face was red, and his eyes were dark and shiny, like onyx. He had big horns on each side of his head, and his hair was long and as black as the night. "How dare you take these souls to the sun?" he growled. "They are the food I feed upon!"

I replied, "Those souls are not yours to feed upon. Those souls belong to the sun."

The demon laughed in my face, loud, maniacal, and mocking. His hot, fiery breath burned my cheeks. Suddenly, he jumped toward me—but instead of running away, I wrapped my arms around him and said to myself, *I will forgive this demon, even if it's the last thing I do.* I held him tight, and with all the love I could muster, I forgave him for his actions toward me and the spirits he was feeding upon.

It was only then that I realized the demon was me.

I opened my eyes, and I no longer saw the demon. Instead, I saw myself as a little boy. I saw myself going through all the stages of my life, from a five-year-old to an eight-year-old to a twelve-year-old to a fifteen-year-old to a seventeen-year-old and finally to the age of twenty-four, which is the age I was at the time. I looked at myself and said, "Thank you for coming back for me. All those souls that you sent to the sun—the ones that were waiting to enter the cave to feed the demon—were you. They were your future self." I awoke from the dream and realized that I was still in the hospital.

I opened my eyes, and I could see just a little bit of light. Excited, I rolled out of bed and felt my way to the bathroom to look at myself in the mirror. I could see a very faint version of myself in the mirror, and I knew that I was going to get my eyesight back in full.

Remembering my dream, I told myself, *I forgive you. I forgive you for any pain you may have caused me.*

I knew at that moment that I was truly the love of my life—the one person on this planet for whom I was completely responsible. I could blame and accuse the love of my life, or I could do everything in my power to make that person happy and support him in becoming well. The choice was mine—and had been all along.

The Practice of Forgiveness

My father once said, "We are the only living creatures on this earth that punish ourselves a thousand times for the same mistake." If I hadn't been blinded and then had that dream about the demon, I might have spent my whole life punishing myself for my former meth addiction. Every time I had a health problem related to those years in the underworld, I would have gone into a dark cave of self-blame. Instead, my episode of blindness served as a turning point, showing me the magic that could happen when I supported the love of my life instead of going against myself.

When you or someone you love makes a mistake, allow the natural consequences to unfold and then move on. What good are you going to do by wallowing in shame, or forcing someone else to wallow in shame? What good are you doing by playing the role of captor, keeping yourself or others imprisoned in the confines of an old mistake? What would happen if you stopped playing prison guard and let those captives free?

Remember, you are the love of your life. No one else can take care of you the way you can. No one fully knows you the way you do, and no one can love you the way you can love yourself. By practicing forgiveness for yourself, you send your soul to the sun instead of confining it to a cave—and allow the love of your life to flourish.

Exercise: Flying to the Sun

Punishing ourselves for the same mistake over and over can feel so familiar that we don't even realize we're doing it. In this exercise, I invite you to bring this pattern into your conscious awareness so that you can set it free.

First, think of an action or decision you regret, and for which you still scold or punish yourself on a regular basis. How many days, months, or years has this punishment been going on?

Next, set a date sometime within the next two weeks at which your self-punishment for this mistake will be complete. Write it on your calendar. This is the day on which you will let yourself fly to the sun.

Until this day arrives, give yourself permission to scold yourself as much as you like.

When the day comes for this self-punishment to end, dance, shake, cry, or do anything else that provides you with an experience of release. As you do so, imagine that this part of your soul has been released from the cave and is flying into the sun.

Your sentence is now over. You are free.

Exercise: The Wound That Heals

While it can be uncomfortable to be sick or injured, these periods of being robbed of our normal functioning can be precious opportunities to rest, reflect, and engage in inner work.

The next time you are sick or injured, take a few minutes to simply be still and watch your thoughts.

What is it like to experience the world in this quieter way? Who are you when you're not doing your regular activities or playing your habitual role?

Does it feel peaceful to abandon your normal activities for a while, or do you feel restless, bored, or even worthless?

Continue observing yourself as these emotions settle. What happens when you let them pass? What lies beyond your familiar ideas about who and what you are? Can you find contentment in bare existence?

Return to this process throughout the day, allowing your period of illness to contain the seeds of healing.

12

The Fallen Messenger

One hundred percent faith will guide you back home.
—Madre Sarita

Even after the awakening I had when I was blind, my progress continued to be nonlinear. Domestication is a powerful force, and although we know what we need to do, it can still take time to build up the courage to do it. I soldiered on in my marriage with Lynn, unable to face the "failure" of leaving—and unwilling to give up the convenient excuse for my unhappiness. My addiction to suffering was proving to be very hard to kick.

Every day, I looked out for my next "fix" of suffering, finding it in drama, blame, and tales of victimhood—and as long as I had my marriage, it was never too hard to find that fix.

One day, eight or nine months into our marriage, Lynn and I were in the kitchen having a drunken argument. We were going around and around in circles, each of us finding the words that would hurt the other person the most. I wanted her to know how terrible she was making me feel. I wanted to hurt her by showing her how badly she was hurting me. I grabbed a knife and started stabbing myself in the stomach, intent on showing Lynn and everyone else in the world just how much pain I was in.

She called my father. He and my brother Miguel arrived quickly and rushed me to the hospital. As I lay in the emergency room, my stomach bleeding from the gaping wound I had inflicted upon myself, and my father standing beside me with tears streaming down his cheeks, I couldn't stop thinking about Elmo, my best friend who had died in the car crash six years earlier. I had vowed that his death would not be in vain—that I was going to change my life and make a difference in the world. Now, here I was, lying in the hospital after I'd tried to throw that life away.

My father placed his hand on my forehead, and I looked deep into his eyes. I saw a brilliant white light coming from my father's eyes and streaming into mine, and at that moment my entire life began flashing through my mind.

I saw myself at fifteen years old, hanging out on the beach in Tijuana with my friends. Suddenly, a huge wave grabbed me, pulled me into the water, and tossed me around like a rag doll. The current was so strong, I couldn't swim out. I struggled and struggled until I finally gave up. I felt myself sinking and knew I was drowning, so I began praying to Mother Ocean. *If you let me go, I promise to spend my life serving others by doing what my family does*, I said silently.

At that moment, the waters calmed down, and my friend saw me floating on top of the water. He ran into the ocean, grabbed my body, and pulled me onto the beach. I began coughing and gasping, so grateful for life—for the simple gift of breathing air.

Next, I began experiencing memories of my life in the deep hell of drug addiction. I saw my family and friends doing everything they could to help me, but I continued to push them away. I lived in my bedroom, and my life consisted of being high, going through horrible withdrawals, and doing what I needed to do to score my next fix. The paranoia was so intense that I hid from everyone and everything. I spent days alone, ignoring everyone. I wouldn't eat or sleep. My mind raced with creative ideas, none of which would be fulfilled while I was trapped in my addiction.

My vision now skipped forward to my unhealthy relationship with Lynn. I saw the huge fight Lynn and I had had that very day, both of us drunk beyond comprehension and using terrible words and manipulation to hurt one another. In slow motion, the event replayed itself. I saw myself walking to the kitchen, pulling a steak knife from the drawer, and stabbing myself in the stomach, not once but twice. I truly wanted to die. I felt there was no point in living anymore.

As I lay on the operating table, I opened my eyes and saw a sheet over my head. My first thought was, *Am I dead?* But then I heard someone sneeze, and I said, "Salud." The doctor laughed and said, "Oh, you're awake." They had just finished stitching up my stab wound, and the doctor pronounced that I was going to be okay.

When I was rolled out of recovery and into my hospital room, my father was waiting for me. He didn't say a word; he just looked at me. I started to apologize, and he said, "Why did you do that, Son?"

I began to make up excuses for why I would stab myself. "I did it because you and Mom divorced. I did it because of the drug addiction. I did it because of Lynn."

My father stopped me and said, "No, Son. You did it because you were stupid. Now hit yourself in the head."

I did as he said. Then he said, "Now do it again." After a few hits, I stopped. I was tired of hitting myself. It hurt. My father said, "See? Now you are no longer stupid."

Taking Responsibility

While my father's words may seem unkind or even harsh, he was teaching me something I already knew deep down: I alone was responsible for my actions. No person from my past had reached out and stabbed me in the stomach—I had done that. Plenty of people had been through experiences similar to mine, or even worse ones, and they hadn't done what I had done. Therefore, my actions weren't the inevitable result of the things that had happened to me, but a *choice* I had made.

When we are children, many of us learn to blame others out of fear of being punished. We quickly realize that if we say, "I didn't break the lamp, the cat jumped on the table and knocked it over!" we can avoid responsibility, preserving an image of ourselves as perfectly good, upstanding citizens who do no wrong. Unfortunately, many of us carry this childish habit into adulthood. We don't love ourselves enough to accept our imperfections, so we look for someone else to blame, whether that's a partner, coworker, neighbor, or relative.

Another reason we blame others for our problems is because we're terrified we don't have the skill or strength to heal our wounds, mend our bad habits, and step into a new life. As long as someone else is responsible, we don't even need to try. After all, what if we try to improve our lives and fail? It feels much safer to tell ourselves that the situation is outside of our control than face the possibility that we need to grow and change.

However, when we take responsibility for our lives, the addiction to suffering begins to weaken. All the drama and chaos that came from playing the victim and blaming others withers away with nothing to feed it. Happiness comes more easily, and life is revealed as a precious gift that is ours to shape as we will.

When I left the hospital that day, I was determined that from that point on, I would take responsibility for my actions. But would it be enough to save my marriage?

Exercise: Someone Says

To learn a new skill, it is sometimes helpful to practice the opposite. For one day, I invite you to act as though all of your actions had been performed by someone else. For example, when you make a cup of coffee, remark to yourself, "Somebody made me coffee!" When you feel stressed out or let down, think, "Somebody is feeling my emotions!" When you can't find your car keys, say, "Somebody lost my keys!"

Notice how funny it is to pretend that anybody but you is responsible for these conditions in your life.

Return to this exercise whenever you find yourself slipping into the habit of looking for external causes for your experiences.

Exercise: Releasing the Scapegoat

Think of a problem in your life for which you have a designated scapegoat. For example, maybe you tell yourself that you can't get healthy and fit until your partner stops being such a couch potato.

Next, make a list of all the people you know who face a similar obstacle but achieve their goal nonetheless. Is the scapegoat really the reason for your problem? Or would your problem still be there even if the scapegoat changed?

What is it like to realize that the thing holding you back isn't the scapegoat, but rather your habit of blame?

13

The Burning Candle

If the candle is still burning there is still time to change your life, no matter what age you are.
—Abuelita Leonarda

Shortly after my suicide attempt, my father was scheduled to go on a one-week teaching trip to Teotihuacan with a small group of his apprentices. He didn't want to let me out of his sight so soon after I had tried to kill myself, so he decided to take me with him.

I was glad to go. I needed his love and guidance so badly at that time in my life. Indeed, they were the only things keeping me alive. My father seemed to have infinite patience for me no matter how many times I went astray. Even though some of his students disapproved of me, and even though some of our family members said I was nothing but trouble, he always kept me under his wing, teaching me everything he knew. Not only that, but I had finally *accepted* him as my teacher—not a friend, not a parent, but as my spiritual teacher. This acceptance transformed everything.

One night during the retreat, he spoke to his apprentices about telepathy. "Telepathy doesn't mean hearing another person's thoughts," he explained. "It means being connected to that person through *energy*." He looked at each one of us in turn. "I want all of you to know that you will always be connected to me. It's not going to be through voice. It's not going to be through language. It's going to be through energy."

Earlier in the book, I explained that *nagual* is the Toltec word for shaman. But like many words in English, *nagual* has another meaning: it refers to the life force energy. This concept doesn't have an exact English translation but can be described through metaphor. For instance, let's compare being human to a computer, where the hardware—the keyboard, mouse, CPU, monitor, and other pieces—is like your physical body, and the software that governs what functions the computer can do is like your mind. But the computer needs something else to function, and that's electricity. This is what we mean by *nagual*; it is the energy that gives life to your body and mind and is something that we all possess in equal measure.

Now, the retreat was over. My father was flying home to San Diego, and I was going home to Malibu. As we waited in the Oaxaca airport, he reminded me of what he'd said on the retreat. "There is no separation between us. Your energy will always be connected to mine, wherever we go."

Like a child, I held his hand tight, not wanting to let go. I was like a baby bird, cautious and unready to fly on my own. The trip to Teotihuacan had been healing for me, but I was afraid to go back to my life in Malibu and confront the mess of my marriage. I wanted to stay near my father. I had a strange feeling that I would never see him again—and no matter what he said, I didn't want to contemplate a future in which my only connection to him was energetic. I needed a real, physical dad who could talk to me. Still, I gave him a big hug and proceeded to the plane.

That night, I was sound asleep in my bed in Malibu when the phone rang. It was my grandmother telling me to come to San Diego because my father had just had a heart attack. When I arrived at the hospital, for the first time in my life, I saw my father very weak, with tubes connected to him everywhere. I completely lost my composure and ran to his side, crying, "Father, you cannot leave me! Father, this can't be happening."

With all the strength he could muster, my father sat straight up in bed. He gave me a piercing look, and said, "Is this the way you are going to celebrate the death of your father? No, Son. Leave the room and come back once you've collected yourself."

Shocked and saddened, I left the room and walked down the hall of the hospital. I began remembering all that I had forgotten—my father's teachings on life and death, attachment and detachment, and the permanence of our nagual energy. I began to see my selfishness. I was going to spoil the last moments of this great man's bodily existence with my own drama. I was participating in such suffering and remorse over my father's death, and he wasn't even dead yet.

Once I was certain that I was thinking straight, I returned to my father's room, took his hand, and said, "I am with you now, Pops. I am with you."

My father said, "Welcome back home, my son. Now I want to give you my last teaching.

"You are going to observe suffering like you have never seen before. Your mother, your aunts, and your uncles are going to be in so much pain, they may say things they don't really mean. But remember, it is not coming from their truth. It is coming from their immense suffering. They are going to make up stories about what I would like from you, about what I would expect from you. But remember, Son, the only thing I want from you is for you to live your life in pure joy and happiness. I want you to do what you love to do and to always be in love with life. Do you understand what I'm telling you, Son?"

I replied, "Yes, Father," and he said right back, "Okay, good. Now get out of the room. I have many others I need to talk to before I go."

That was the last time I spoke to my father before he went into a nine-week coma. Everything he had predicted began happening. Everyone was crying and sad, but I was doing as my father suggested. I was joking around, attempting to bring some joy into the household, telling funny stories and memories of my father that brought me happiness. My elders began telling me many things that my father would wish from me: "Jose, your father would want you to do this; your father suggested you do that." I even got a very emotional, "Jose, it is all your fault that your father is in this condition," and "What's wrong with you, Jose? Why are you so happy? You need therapy!"

Some of my relatives blamed me for my father's heart attack: I had put him through so much stress, what with my drug addiction, suicide attempt, and crazy life. If I had just held it together, this never would've happened to him. I felt angry when I heard those comments, but I remembered what my father had told me in the hospital room, and I was thankful for his message. I knew that my relatives were speaking out of hurt and suffering—and that there was no need to respond in kind.

You Don't Have Time

One of the most powerful lessons that illness and close calls with death can teach you is that you don't have time! You don't have time to suffer, you don't have time to wallow in sadness, and you don't have time to be a victim. *You don't have time.* Spend your time enjoying life, making beautiful memories, and forgiving those who have hurt you. Otherwise, when death knocks on your door, you will realize in a flash how much time you have wasted, and you will beg the Angel of Death for one more chance.

How many hours of our lives have we spent in gossip, drama, and blame? How many evenings have we sat up late, fuming about the latest injustice at work or the outrageous thing our neighbor said, or plotting our revenge for some petty slight? At the end of our lives, will this look like time well spent, or like an astonishing waste of our sojourn on this planet?

Life is so full of gifts. We have the beautiful planet, the sun and rain, plants and animals, and the presence of other human beings with all their wisdom and their flaws. We can choose to transform this heaven into a hell, or we can live our lives in pure joy and happiness, knowing they can end at any time.

After nine weeks, my father woke up from his coma. He had to learn many things over again—how to walk, how to speak. He even had to learn to recognize the faces of his loved ones. I was so grateful that I could once more speak to him, listen to his words, and learn from him. Every moment with him felt precious—just as it had always been.

Exercise: The Wonder of Nature

As humans, our minds are in the habit of dreaming up problems all day, while scarcely noticing the beautiful life unfolding all around us.

Every day for a week, spend at least five minutes simply sitting outside and watching nature.

See the leaves swaying, the water rippling, or the sun setting behind the clouds.

Realize that *this* life is just as real as the life inside your head—some might say more real.

Practice tuning out your thoughts, and tuning into this larger life that always surrounds you, and which is always beautiful.

After the week is over, I bet you will want to continue this practice.

Exercise: Genuine Joy

Some of us keep a bucket list filled with things we'd like to do before we die. But imagine if that list contained a single goal: being genuinely joyful for a few moments every day.

Every morning for one week, I want you to spend five minutes reflecting on something that brings you joy, or finding joy in the present moment without reason, and allow yourself to fully enjoy the experience.

Think the words, *I am truly joyful in this moment.*

Rest in this joyfulness for a few minutes before you begin the work of your day. The more you notice and acknowledge joy, the more joy will appear in your life.

Like the previous exercise on nature, you may find this practice so valuable you will want to continue it after the week is over.

14

The Courage to Act

*If you say you can't do it, you will not
do it. Be aware of what you agree to.*
—don Miguel Ruiz

After his heart attack, my father was left with only 16 percent of his heart capacity. He was also in agonizing pain and had very little energy. In fact, when he was being released from the hospital, the doctor told him, "Miguel, you will have to spend the rest of your days just relaxing in your home, attending movies and dinners, and doing very little activity." My father replied, "Yes, doctor," but he was holding one hand behind his back with his fingers crossed.

Once the doctor left, he gathered us around his bed and declared, "There is no way I am going to lie around waiting for the Angel of Death to come for me. I will go out and find the Angel of Death while I continue to do what I love to do." And my father did just that. He continued to travel around the United States and Mexico, teaching the principles of our Toltec tradition to anyone who wanted to learn. He never allowed anyone to see his incredible pain or loss of energy. I was lucky enough to accompany him on many of these trips, teaching alongside him and walking my own spiritual path.

These trips with my father were a time of immense learning for me. I was continually inspired by the way he made ancient Toltec teachings relevant and applicable to a huge and diverse audience, and the way he inspired every one of his apprentices to make deep and lasting changes in their lives. I was also humbled by his insistence that, rather than strive to be a carbon copy of him, I find my own relationship to the teachings, and to the act of being a teacher. It felt good to know that, as much as I loved and respected my father, I didn't have to form myself in his image; indeed, he encouraged me to be myself.

A few years after his heart attack, my father received a heart transplant. After the operation, the doctor came into his room and asked if my father would mind if they studied his heart. They were surprised that he had survived, doing what he did, with only 16 percent of his heart capacity. My father, being a medical doctor himself, replied, "Don't waste your time, doctor. It's not in the heart; it's in the will."

As for myself, I was struggling to find the will I needed—the will to leave my marriage to Lynn, which had now been dragging on for close to nine years. Again and again, it seemed we were just on the brink of solving our problems, and I would convince myself to stay. After all, I didn't want to quit five minutes before my miracle. But the bigger picture that was emerging was not one of healing, but of entrenched unhappiness and unresolvable differences on both sides.

Luckily, I had my father and grandmother to help me find my way. One day, I was assisting Madre Sarita in one of her classes, acting as translator. The class had just ended, the students had filed out, and I was sitting in a corner of the room. Lynn and I had had yet another argument the night before, and I was hoping to ask for Madre Sarita's advice.

But before I could open my mouth, my grandmother looked right at me. "Jose," she said, "I was almost seventy years old before I decided to stop giving anyone the power to determine my happiness and peace. You're still young. It's time to take your power back. Love and respect yourself enough to detach from this marriage, and love and respect Lynn enough to let her go."

Her words were filled with the kind of love and ferocity that only a grandmother can provide. I knew right away that she was speaking the truth. For years now, I had been too afraid to give up on my image of the loyal husband who devotes himself to one woman for the rest of his life, no matter how unhappy he is. I had given all my power to this image—sacrificed myself to it, like a goat on an altar. And for what? This sacrifice hadn't made Lynn any happier. It hadn't given my life meaning. It hadn't helped my family. So what was the sacrifice for?

I knew deep down that the real reason I'd stayed in my marriage for so long was my addiction to suffering. I was so used to feeling bad that I'd almost forgotten how to do anything other than complain. For so many years, waiting around for the Angel of Death to claim me just felt like the way things were. But now that I had stopped using drugs and I had begun to look within and do the inner work that was necessary, my addiction to suffering was slowly fading away. I realized that I could take another path.

"Thank you, Grandma," I said. "Thank you for telling me the truth. I've known this for a long time, and I'm ready to step into my power, just like you say."

Wise Action

Many times, we hang back from taking an important step in our lives because we're afraid of hurting someone. We tell ourselves the other person will be devastated by our action, and so we stay where we are, not realizing that devastation can also be wrought, albeit more slowly and quietly, through *inaction*. If you're unhappy in a relationship, what are the odds that your partner is happy? And is it really true that their happiness depends on you? If that were the case, they would have literally no happy memories until the moment they met you — but that's never the case!

The truth is, it's often our own fear of change that keeps us stuck, not the real or imagined fragility of the people around us. *We're* the ones who are fragile, or at least believe ourselves to be — the ones who think we won't be able to handle the intense emotions or logistical challenges of making big changes in our lives. Yet when we finally take that leap, we realize that we have more strength than we assumed—and so does the other person.

Often, truly loving and respecting someone means recognizing that their life is much bigger than their relationship with you. Their life has possibilities you can't even imagine—futures you couldn't dream up in a million years. The word *Toltec* means artist, and in the Toltec tradition we emphasize respect for the art of others—even for the art they haven't created yet. If you think another person's life will be ruined by a necessary step that you're taking, chances are you're underestimating that person—not to mention the extraordinary creative potential of life itself.

As long as I chose to complain about my marriage instead of ending it, neither Lynn nor I would be free to pursue the lives that would make us happy. For years, I had put all my energy into complaining. Now it was time to step into my true power and find the courage to take the action I'd been avoiding.

Exercise: Owning Your Emotions

The next time you find yourself making an excuse not to act based on another person's probable reaction, try rephrasing it to own those emotions in yourself.

For example, if you think, *I can't quit my job because my partner will be disappointed*, try out the phrase, *If I quit my job, I'll be disappointed.*

Next, take a moment to feel the emotion in question. Is this emotion really that bad? Are you really going to put your whole life on hold just because you're afraid of feeling it?

How does it feel to own your emotions about a big decision instead of projecting them onto someone else?

Exercise: Expanding Your Imagination

When you're contemplating a tough decision, it's normal for the mind to provide you with detailed fantasies and predictions of what, exactly, will happen. These negative predictions can distract us from the fact that life is vast and we don't actually know every last possibility.

The next time you find yourself holding off on an important action in your life, take five minutes to visualize some *positive* outcomes. Let your imagination run wild. Maybe your relationship becomes better than ever if you make this change; maybe a new opportunity falls into your lap that could never have happened in your old life.

During this visualization, truly imagine that you are the artist of your life—the one who decides on all the colors, shapes, and experiences. What would it be like to assign yourself that power?

Return to this practice whenever you think you "know" the outcome of your decision.

15

The Eternal Honeymoon

*Before you enter any relationship, become
aware of what level of happiness or
suffering the person is dreaming, because
that will be the dream you are entering.*
—don Miguel Ruiz & Barbara Emrys

When I approached Lynn to end our marriage after nine years together, she was defensive and hurt. "How can you leave me after everything we've been through?" she cried. "I love you so much."

"I love you too," I replied. "But it's time to move on. We'll both be happier, healthier people if we're not married anymore."

The first year after the divorce was difficult. Even though I knew that I'd done the right thing,

I still had to contend with feelings of guilt and failure. Lynn and I continued to talk on the phone and would meet now and then, and these conversations were often painful, as both of us would quickly get pulled into unsolvable questions about what went wrong in our relationship and who or what was to blame. We also felt sad about the good times we had shared, which were now in the past.

But one day, many months after we split up, Lynn called me. "Jose, I want to say thank you for ending things. Since we got divorced, I've come to so many realizations about who I am and how I've been sabotaging my own healing, and I've made so many positive changes in my life. I hope someday you find someone new and fall in love again, because you deserve to be happy."

I could tell by the sound of her voice that she was speaking from a place of truth. It felt so good to know that the hard decision I'd made really had been the best thing for both of us. Now we could both blossom into our full potential. Even though our marriage had been full of turmoil, I realized that I was grateful for every moment of it. Lynn and I had been part of each other's journeys; in our own way, we had done our best and spurred one another to grow. Just like my teenage years in Tijuana, my time with Lynn had been a form of shamanic initiation. Now that I had passed through that experience, there was nothing to regret.

I liked the idea of dating again, but I knew that if I wasn't careful, I would jump into a new relationship and repeat the same old patterns all over again. In *The Four Agreements*, my father wrote, "You attract into your life someone who abuses you just a little less than you abuse yourself." In other words, our unconscious beliefs about what we deserve can lead us to accept abuse from others, especially in intimate relationships. As long as you are abusing yourself even a little bit, you create an opening for other people to abuse you too because you've already decided that it's okay.

I realized that this phenomenon had been at play in my relationship with Lynn. At the time we'd gotten married, I didn't know how to be kind to myself, and I certainly didn't know how to let anyone else be kind to me. I didn't know how to comfort myself, and I didn't know how to let anyone comfort me. I didn't know how to be honest with myself, and I didn't know how to let anyone be honest with me. If I didn't take care of these things inside myself, I would continue to attract partners who treated me just a little bit less badly.

I took a year off from teaching to work on myself. Slowly, I began to heal. I started eating healthy foods, I stopped drinking, and I lost over fifty pounds. I spent hours meditating, listening to music, and playing with my dog, cultivating happiness on the inside. To my amazement, I realized that I really enjoyed spending time with myself. Jose was a pretty nice person to be around; I liked him a lot. I certainly didn't feel like abusing him anymore, or allowing anybody else to abuse him, either.

I look back on this period of my life as my era of becoming an adult rattlesnake. Finally, after all these years, I was shedding another skin. When I had married Lynn, I was barely out of my teens: an overgrown child looking for a mother to take care of him, and against whom he could rebel. Now, I was stepping into life as a full-grown adult, with an adult's choices to make about my future. I was no longer a baby rattlesnake, releasing all my poison at the slightest hint of a threat, but a mature one with the newfound wisdom of restraint.

As I felt my old skin falling away, I had a wonderful realization: I am the only person I am always going to have. Everyone else is going to leave me in one way or another. This is a simple fact of nature. And if I'm the only person who's going to be there twenty-four hours a day until the moment I die, I had better have a good relationship with myself.

Up until that point in my life, I thought that a grand romance with an ideal woman was going to be the most important relationship I had. Now, it struck me that I was already on an eternal honeymoon with myself. That honeymoon could be full of love, tenderness, and adventure regardless of whether or not I ever married again, or even dated anyone. And if and when I did have new relationships, I could be certain that they would be characterized by love and trust, because those were the qualities I had cultivated within myself.

Giving What You Seek

Sometimes it feels like we're all searching for something outside of ourselves to bring us happiness—something to save us or bring us peace. We seek this salvation from our partners, friends, and relatives. We seek it from teachers and gurus, at workshops and on retreats. Yet the person whose love and acceptance we need most is standing right there in the mirror. Only you can give yourself the very deepest experience of being loved, because only you can open your heart to receive this love—nobody else can do it for you.

When you realize that *you* are the love of your life, life becomes wonderful. After all, you get to spend twenty-four hours a day with your soulmate—the person who is more deeply attuned to your mental, physical, and emotional needs than anyone else on this planet. You don't need to cling to friendships or relationships to the point of suffocating them, because even if that person goes away, you'll still have yourself. And when you do make new friends or fall in love with a partner, you'll have so much more to give them because you've perfected the art of being generous and kind to yourself.

Throughout my life, there were many, many times when somebody who loved me very much tried to save me or give me peace, but I didn't love myself enough to receive it. My father and grandmother, Mama Gaya, my extended family, and all of my friends poured out love for me. Yet I could only receive their love at a rate equivalent to the love I gave myself. If I only gave myself a little love, I could only receive a fraction of the love that was given to me. Therefore, the only way to receive the love I craved was to give it to myself first.

If you have a hard time receiving love, the solution is to fall in love with yourself the same way you would fall in love with a new partner. Show a sense of wonder toward yourself. Be curious about this incredible body and mind you've been given. Notice what makes you happy. See only the best in yourself, and reframe your flaws as areas of potential. Most important, refuse to ever go against yourself in your thoughts, words, or actions. You are here to encourage, inspire, and support yourself, not to bring yourself down. This simple realization changes everything.

It took me a long time to get to this place—my entire life, in fact. But now that I have befriended the love of my life, I know that I will never again suffer the way I used to. This phase of my initiation is now complete, and from now on I am a messenger of unconditional love.

Exercise: Mirror Ritual

Every morning, spend one minute smiling at yourself in the mirror. If you like, you can place a hand on one cheek in a gesture of deep tenderness.

Pretend you are meeting a wonderful new person for the first time—a person with whom you'll be spending the rest of your life.

As you gaze at this person, wish them happiness, love, and peace on this day and always.

If this exercise seems hard or silly to you, that's a cue that you really need to do it. I mean this. Love yourself like you love your parent, child, lover, or whomever is the most important person in the world to you outside yourself.

Exercise: Dazzling Yourself

When we fall in love, we take extra care with our clothes and grooming, eager to dazzle our prospective mate. What if we took the same care in getting dressed just to spend time with ourselves?

One day a week, make a point of wearing your favorite clothes and jewelry even if there's no fancy occasion to justify it. If you enjoy things like makeup and fragrances, use those too.

Notice how good it feels to make yourself beautiful, even if it's just for your own enjoyment. Why do you need another person present to make this pleasure worthwhile?

Conclusion

Spirituality is one side. Humanity is another side. If you ignore the humanity and only do spirituality, that's nonsense. Once we're born as human, we have to care about humanity.
—Swami Kaleshwar

The events in this book are now long in the past. When I think back on them, I often feel amazement that they happened at all. Was I really that lost teenager in Tijuana, exposing myself to so much danger and refusing the help of my family and friends? Was I really that shy twenty-year-old who started shaking uncontrollably the first time I got to speak in front of a large audience? Was I really that young husband in Malibu, rubbing shoulders with celebrities and sneaking off to the taco truck just to feel normal again?

At this point in my life, I've shed my skin many times, and will surely shed many more skins before I leave this earth. As I grow older, I've come to appreciate the simple things in life: walking my dog, listening to music, eating vegan food, and going to my favorite coffeeshops. I spend time with my father and brothers and treasure the bond we share; other times, I chat on the phone with old friends from Tijuana, remembering the good times and the bad. Both of my grandmothers and Mama Gaya have passed away; their ashes sit on my altar, and their wisdom lives on in my memory. I meditate every morning and evening, and do my best to take care of the precious life that has been entrusted to me—my own.

Sometimes I run into an old friend and after catching up they say to me, "Jose, your life has become so boring!" In fact, I am the happiest I've ever been. When you fall in love with life, you don't need danger and drama to keep you busy. Simply enjoying the beautiful gifts of planet earth is enough.

If I had to sum up my spiritual practice in one word, it would be "respect." Respect for my life; respect for all people; respect for all traditions. I'm not here to change anyone, convert anyone, gain followers, or build a cult. I'm here to create my artwork and express my love, while respecting the love and artistry of everyone around me. The practice of respect has opened my eyes to the infinite ways that divinity expresses itself, and to see the divinity in all things. By respecting everything, I can appreciate everything—and I've found that this is a very beautiful way to move through life.

I truly believe in the religious idea of resurrection, but instead of a rare and miraculous event, I believe that this process happens over and over again over the course of a single lifetime. We get hurt or have a near-death experience or just decide we need to make a change. Every time we detach from something in this life, we are in a position to resurrect ourselves and make our life something new—just like the rattlesnake, who sheds his skin and moves on.

These days, there are moments when I get a tickle in my brain—a lingering symptom of my former meth addiction. This tickle reminds me of all the times I survived the crazy hells I put myself in. It makes me grateful to be alive. I still have all the memories, but I have learned to stop using them against myself. Instead, I use them to remind myself of how precious life really is. I use them to remind myself that I am still alive and that I have each day to make my life one that I can be proud of. Each new day is an opportunity to explore my truth and become the person I would truly love to spend the rest of my life with.

Remember, your heart is always celebrating life because it is always beating. Take care of the love of your life; use this precious opportunity to create your own masterpiece of art; and never, ever be afraid to shed your skin.

—don Jose Ruiz
June 2024

About the Authors

Don Jose Ruiz is a nagual (Toltec shaman) in the Eagle Knights lineage, and the son of don Miguel Ruiz, author of *The Four Agreements*. He is the author of *The Wisdom of the Shamans*, *The Medicine Bag*, *Shamanic Power Animals*, and *The Shaman's Path to Freedom*, and the coauthor of *The Fifth Agreement*.

Tami Hudman is an artist and author. She resides in Salt Lake City, Utah.

San Antonio, TX
www.hierophantpublishing.com